BIKEPACKING
— IN THE —
CANADIAN
ROCKIES

RYAN CORREY

RMB

For information on purchasing bulk quantities of this book, or to obtain media excerpts, please visit rmbooks.com and select the "Contact" tab.

RMB | Rocky Mountain Books Ltd.
rmbooks.com
@rmbooks
facebook.com/rmbooks

Cataloguing data available from Library and Archives Canada
ISBN 9781771602372 (softcover)
ISBN 9781771602389 (electronic)

Interior design by Colin Parks
Cover photo by Jeff Bartlett, taken along the High Rockies route

Printed and bound in Canada

We would like to also take this opportunity to acknowledge the traditional territories upon which we live and work. In Calgary, Alberta, we acknowledge the Niitsítapi (Blackfoot) and the people of the Treaty 7 region in Southern Alberta, which includes the Siksika, the Piikuni, the Kainai, the Tsuut'ina and the Stoney Nakoda First Nations, including Chiniki, Bearpaw, and Wesley First Nations. The City of Calgary is also home to Métis Nation of Alberta, Region III. In Victoria, British Columbia, we acknowledge the traditional territories of the Lkwungen (Esquimalt, and Songhees), Malahat, Pacheedaht, Scia'new, T'Sou-ke and W̱SÁNEĆ (Pauquachin, Tsartlip, Tsawout, Tseycum) peoples.

We acknowledge the financial support of the Government of Canada through the Canada Book Fund and the Canada Council for the Arts, and of the province of British Columbia through the British Columbia Arts Council and the Book Publishing Tax Credit.

Disclaimer
The actions described in this book may be considered inherently dangerous activities. Individuals undertake these activities at their own risk. The information put forth in this guide has been collected from a variety of sources and is not guaranteed to be completely accurate or reliable. Many conditions and some information may change owing to weather and numerous other factors beyond the control of the authors and publishers. Individuals or groups must determine the risks, use their own judgment, and take full responsibility for their actions. Do not depend on any information found in this book for your own personal safety. Your safety depends on your own good judgment based on your skills, education, and experience.

It is up to the users of this guidebook to acquire the necessary skills for safe experiences and to exercise caution in potentially hazardous areas. The authors and publishers of this guide accept no responsibility for your actions or the results that occur from another's actions, choices, or judgments. If you have any doubt as to your safety or your ability to attempt anything described in this guidebook, do not attempt it.

Contents

FOREWORD

The Emergence of Bikepacking

When I met Ryan Correy at the Alberta Bikes Conference at the Canmore Nordic Centre in September 2016, I immediately knew I had found a kindred spirit — even if he did grow up playing hockey, while baseball was the game of my youth. Ryan and I were same-day presenters at the conference, which centred on bicycle tourism. The title of my morning presentation was "Map It and They Will Come: The Genesis of the Great Divide Mountain Bike Route." Later in the day, Ryan spoke on "The Emergence of Bikepacking in Canada." Early in his talk, the aspiring guidebook writer held up a copy of my own guidebook — *Cycling the Great Divide* — and asked me, sitting in the audience, if I would sign it for him.

"Sure will," I said.

We share a similar passionate mission, Ryan and I: Get people, young and old, out on bicycles and into the backcountry. Camp out, inhale the fresh air, encounter wild animals. Or, as John Muir wrote in *Our National Parks*, "Climb the mountains and get their good tidings. Nature's peace will flow into you as sunshine flows into trees."

A few months later, in February 2017, Ryan interviewed me over the phone for his podcast at bikepack.ca. I was flattered when he wrapped up the session by saying he considers me a mentor.

True, I did research and map the Great Divide Mountain Bike Route back in the mid-1990s. However, I must admit that I am surprised, perhaps more than anyone, at the profound impact the trail has had on the bicycling/ outdoor universe.

The road to creating the route was hilly and circuitous, but the theory behind it was simple: let's pour bicycle touring and mountain biking into an empty blender, turn it on, and see what we come up with. Following is how we arrived at the empty blender point.

The Great Divide was and is a project of the Missoula, Montana–based Adventure Cycling Association. Adventure Cycling began life in 1974 as Bikecentennial, forming when a group of visionary young bicycle tourists decided to throw a two-wheeled, 200th-birthday bash for the American Bicentennial, and invite the world to bicycle across the United States.

My future wife, Nancy, and I, having caught the bicycle-touring bug and ridden from Seattle to northeast Wisconsin the summer of 1974, became involved in the Bikecentennial project, working the western half of the TransAmerica Bicycle Trail during the summer of 1976. During that summer, nearly 5,000 individuals from throughout the U.S. and far beyond pedalled all or portions of the Oregon-to-Virginia TransAm Trail.

The founders had envisioned Bikecentennial simply as a one-time event. However, North America's growing legion of bicycle enthusiasts wouldn't let the idea go away. Hundreds more, inspired by articles in the press and tales brought home by those who rode in '76, wanted their own shot at pedalling across America.

So, Bikecentennial carried on, but after the big summer was over, Nancy and I went on to other things. When she landed her first teaching job in Troy, Montana, in the early '80s (we were married by this time), I went to work seasonally for the Yaak Ranger District of the Kootenai National Forest. Among my varied duties over those two summers was to survey, via Honda 90 motorcycle, the district's decommissioned roads — that is, roads closed either by gates or "Kelly humps" — to find and document erosional/watershed problems. For me it was an eye-opener. If this one national forest district had so many hundreds of miles of unused gravel roads, other districts must have them too.

In the spring of 1982 I went back to work for Bikecentennial as the assistant tours coordinator. The timing coincided with the exploding popularity of a new style of bicycle, the mountain bike. Nancy and I took right to the fat-tired bikes, riding not only the trails outside Missoula but also on the dirt and gravel roads in the surrounding Lolo National Forest, which were so like the ones I'd discovered in the Kootenai. It didn't take long before I was thinking, "Why not pack up and do some multi-day rides on the mountain bikes? Get off the busy highways and into the backcountry."

One early bikepacking trip — although we weren't yet calling it that — was a five-dayer from the Tri-Basin Divide in southwest Wyoming to Jackson Hole, by way of the Greys River, Salt River, Wind River and Gros Ventre mountain ranges. The trip was fun, hard, a grand adventure, and another real eye-opener.

Although Bikecentennial was best known for the TransAm Trail and other routes following paved roads, we soon started thinking outside the cement-and-asphalt box. A crystallizing moment happened in 1990, when then-executive-director Gary MacFadden and I were having lunch at a Mexican restaurant in Missoula. Brainstorming for new ideas, one of us said to the other something like, "Let's map a mountain-bike route along the Continental Divide from Canada to Mexico."

What a concept! But as intriguing as it sounded, the idea was shelved as the Bikecentennial staff worked on other, more pressing matters. Then, early in 1994, Gary and I were having lunch again, same place. "Mac?" he asked. "Do you remember that long-distance mountain-bike route we discussed a few years back?"

I did, and we agreed the time was right to do it. Why? For one thing, we had just finished adding a decade-long wish list of road routes to the National Bicycle Routes Network. Plus, the concept fit snugly with our new (at the time) name: Adventure Cycling Association.

In the July 1994 *Adventure Cyclist* magazine, we ran a two-page story, written by me, under the bold headline "Ready for the Longest Mountain Bike Trail in the World?" The piece began: "Imagine mountain biking from Canada to Mexico, through some of the most stunning landscapes on earth, along dirt roads and two-tracks reserved for the occasional fisherman's rig, Forest Service pickup truck...and Adventure Cycling mountain biker."

In the story, I explained the origin of our dream of an off-pavement route paralleling the Continental Divide, and why we wanted to make it happen: "Historically, cycling enthusiasts have done one or the other — either loaded up with panniers and camping gear and lit out on the open road or headed into the hills on a mountain bike for a day's ride on dirt. Very few have toured off-pavement carrying a full complement of gear. We want to change that."

The Adventure Cycling staff immediately became excited by the possibilities of this cycling route paralleling the Continental Divide. We pictured riding it as a merging of three activities: bicycle touring, mountain biking and backpacking. This time we did call it "bikepacking." We chose to name the project the Great Divide Mountain Bike Route, in part to distinguish it from the Continental Divide National Scenic Trail, a hiking route composed largely of rugged single-track trails. In planning our strategy, we agreed we would try to avoid tough single tracks, knowing that riding most mountain trails while carrying or pulling a heavy load is prohibitively difficult.

The task of researching the Great Divide fell to me in late 1994. "It's a tough duty, but somebody's gotta do it" became my mantra for the next four years. Still, it was anything but a one-man show. The project quickly captured the imagination of hundreds; consequently, things jelled and got done fast. Dozens of agency personnel and local cycling enthusiasts jumped in to offer help with field reconnaissance. We received great support, monetary and otherwise, from the likes of Travel Montana, REI, Flanagan Motors in Missoula and the Adventure Cycling membership.

So, I spent the snowless months of the next three years — 1995, 1996 and 1997 — plotting the route, via mountain bike and Jeep Cherokee. (The original route was border-to-border in the U.S.; we added the leg from the international border north to Banff in the early 2000s.) And I had plenty of adventures along the way.

Like the time I learned that Jeeps can't swim, by swamping the Cherokee in rain-swollen Rock Creek outside Kremmling, Colorado. I mean stuck, dead in the middle of the waist-deep creek. Getting to "shore" was a challenge, and so was getting the Jeep out of the creek.

And like the day in New Mexico, basically in the middle of nowhere, when I drove through an open roadblock gate sporting an unlatched padlock hanging from the locking mechanism. Fifteen miles later I ran into *another* gate, this one shut and locked. Returning to gate number one, I now found it closed and the padlock clicked shut. I was locked in. I had no cell phone in those days. After about an hour of scratching my head, the solution arrived, strangely, in the form of a very large enforcer-type guy possessing the padlock key. He wore a suit (not often seen in backcountry New Mexico), had a Rocky Balboa build and revealed a bulge in his sport jacket that I figured was a handgun. I know he did not believe I had found the gate unlocked, because it was not supposed to be unlocked. Someone had tampered with it, and he assumed it was me. Unsmilingly, he finally unlocked the gate and set me free. (To this day, I believe I was on public lands. But maybe I misread the map. It's been known to happen.)

During the two decades since mapping the Great Divide, I've been gratified to witness the gradual growth, and finally the boom, in bikepacking. The race following the route, the Tour Divide, has captured a lot of press and attention, drawing a lot of folks into the sport. (Yet, it should be noted that far more people tour the Great Divide than race it.) The emergence of "gravel grinders" — which I prefer to call "gravel fondos" — is another indirect, or maybe even direct, spinoff of the route. Great to see.

By using the Great Divide as a backbone or jumping-off point for new routes in the Canadian Rockies, Ryan is helping to fulfill one of our early hopes: that the Great Divide Mountain Bike Route would become the starting point, literally and figuratively, for new rides, routes and events devised by others.

Good work, man! Thanks for picking up the ball. I look forward to test-riding some of your routes.

— **MICHAEL MCCOY**, FATHER OF THE
GREAT DIVIDE MOUNTAIN BIKE ROUTE

PREFACE

In early 2016, Ryan shared with me his idea of creating a bikepacking guidebook. With his ambitious way in life, it wasn't long before it had blossomed into an all-encompassing undertaking. From the early stages of meticulously poring over maps, to his countless scouting missions into the Alberta and BC backcountry, Ryan poured himself into this project over the next summer and spring.

Crafting this guidebook was, perhaps, a pinnacle project for Ryan, a culmination of his years of cycling, his love of exploring new places by bike, his passion for sharing his experiences with others, and his desire to grow the bikepacking community in Canada.

For all the adventure and ambition these route descriptions reflect, however, the pages ahead cannot fully capture the enormous effort Ryan devoted to this book. They do not tell of the miles ridden to disappointing dead ends, the exhausting climbs to impassable roads, the perseverance of bushwhacking for entire days along overgrown trails, the nasty weather endured, the time away from work and family, and the many hours in front of a computer screen researching historical facts, collating notes on trail conditions and connecting lines on maps.

It is this dedication that makes this guidebook most special to me. It is time and energy that is infinitely more precious knowing it was Ryan's last project.

Ryan fell ill while scouting the last route for this book. In the nine months that followed, while grappling with a shocking diagnosis, chemotherapy and rapidly declining health, he dedicated any energy he could spare to editing and fine-tuning this into a book he would be proud of.

Ryan died on April 27, 2018. It is both a great honour and a bittersweet milestone to have *Bikepacking in the Canadian Rockies* published. I certainly wish Ryan could have seen the finished product. But there is great peace in knowing he spent his last months of health adventuring through the mountains on his bike and living up to his goal in life: to turn his passion into purpose. I hope you experience some of that very passion as you embark on your own adventures and share in Ryan's dream!

— **SARAH HORNBY**

INTRODUCTION

33 Years in the Making,
a Love Affair with the Canadian Rockies

The Rocky Mountains have always been a quick escape. Where I grew up on the outskirts of Calgary, the eastern range was clearly visible from my bedroom window.

I recall hockey tournaments in Canmore, catching fluffy snowflakes outside the Post Hotel in Lake Louise, rustic wood architecture in Jasper, skiing at Nakiska as part of a yearly junior-high retreat, dragging my feet on family hikes in Kananaskis, the smell of composting forest beds along the Bow River, chasing our rambunctious golden retriever through overgrown poplar and sporadic chinook winds on an otherwise frigid afternoon.

My introduction to cycling in the Canadian Rockies was in high school (at the National Sport School), back in 1999. Our phys ed teacher coordinated a three-day tour for a group of mostly hockey misfits along the infamous Icefields Parkway, running 291 km from Jasper to Banff. Having cycled with my father across most of Canada in the three years prior — "Manhood Training," as he called it — I found the daily grind of the grand valley tour came second nature.

Fast-forward a decade to the TransRockies (TR7) stage race in 2009. It was my first year of proper mountain biking, and I had committed to grinding it out from Panorama Ski Hill (just west of the Rockies, in the Purcell Mountains) to Fernie, British Columbia. Barry Mah at Specialized Bicycles kindly sponsored my entry. He and a few others were intrigued to see what "that guy" could pull off: the young man who had turned his back on hockey to cycle 14,000 km around North America in 2002, race 25,000 km from Alaska to Argentina in 2005, and become the youngest Canadian to complete the infamous Race Across America in 2008.

Midway through a respectable fourth-place TR7 finish, I befriended then Rocky Mountain Bicycles rep Keith Brodsky and his riding partner, Alaskan reporter Jill Homer. Homer excitedly inquired after one of the stages if I had heard of a new self-supported mountain bike race called the Tour Divide. "It's right up your alley!" she exclaimed, referring to my ambitious tendencies.

Jill was one of only a handful of women to have completed the epic, still in its infancy.

"Maybe," I said, somewhat intrigued. But that was where the conversation ended.

The following year, in October 2010, I took on a six-day, 20-hour stationary-cycling world record attempt in what was intended to be a unique community engagement event (a more apt description can be found in my autobiography, *A Purpose Ridden*). The physical aftershocks, the worst I have ever experienced, still haunt me: three months of crippling nerve pain, insomnia, muscle atrophy, a loss of fat padding in my feet, fatigued adrenal glands and a terrible bout of depression.

I don't want to die alone

In September 2011 I moved across the country to Ontario to live with an amazing gal I'd met online during my exhausting recovery. "Sarah is perfect... but above all, it's time for a change," I told my co-workers in Sylvan Lake (I had been managing a gym in central Alberta for three years). Achieving a balance in life had begun to take priority over single-minded cycling aspirations.

Hobbled jogs along Lake Ontario emerged as a convenient new way to stay fit. Still, on hikes along the Niagara escarpment, I would catch a glimpse of a single-track trail and be taken back to my days of mountain bike racing at the Canmore Nordic Centre, along the North Saskatchewan River at Edmonton and up and down the windy coulees around Lethbridge. The spin attempt had decimated my fast twitch muscle, I admitted. But the ability to go long and slow, that mental muscle, remained an edge.

Talk of the Tour Divide resurfaces

Envisioning the leadup in my mind's eye, I saw the gate of the Rockies rising steeply from the undeveloped golden grasslands of the Stoney Nakoda Nation. That dramatic scene at the crest of Scott Lake Hill that you see when headed west along the Trans-Canada Highway would take me back to an earlier memory of mountain grandeur: early summer hikes with the family, all that. I saw the bird's-eye view play over and over. And finally, the obscure Divide was reality.

June 8, 2012 — Sarah and I share a nervous parting kiss outside the Banff YWCA

Due to time constraints and a tinge of naivety, experience with a few key pieces of gear had been limited to one (sunny) overnighter back in Ontario. That equipment being my bivouac sleep sack, Garmin GPS and custom Porcelain Rocket bags. "Got three or so weeks to figure it out," I quietly joked amongst a crowd of 116 who were seemingly more experienced.

Cresting a frigid Elk Pass later that afternoon, I learned the critical difference between "waterproof" and "water resistant" as muddy tracks mixed with unseasonal snow. Continuing through the remote Flathead Valley high country of Montana, Idaho, the windy Great Basin in Wyoming and the alpine of Colorado, my outer shell would grow leathery and much the wiser. *Others need to experience this*, I thought, breathing deeply in that rich mountain air.

Soon after returning home from the 21-day sprint to New Mexico, I jumped head-first into planning a supported adventure along the first leg of the route to Whitefish, Montana. Eleven participants signed up from across Canada and the United States. Our "Great Divide Mountain Bike Tour" was touted as a way to experience the Divide with a safety net. In addition to a support crew of four loyal friends, participants had the piece of mind of riding with yours truly, a Tour Divide finisher and recent graduate of the Ecotourism & Outdoor Leadership program at Mount Royal University in Calgary.

Our group met for the first time on August 30, 2013, at the Calgary International Airport. Outside the arrivals terminal, we crammed into a 15-seater passenger van and shuttled three hours south to begin a last-minute reroute to Helena, Montana. Our original track through the Bow Valley had been decimated by flooding one month before (in Canmore, for example, 200 mm of rain fell in just 48 hours). Fortunately, the group's tremendous camaraderie would smooth over our inaugural humps.

Live. Learn. Repeat.

Year 2 saw no issues with the Great Divide. Mind you, we had not yet been able to acquire the appropriate insurance and park permits (and ultimately run a legitimate business). Our cross-border route presented several red flags for the bureaucratic types.

Onward. In June 2015 I returned with fire in my eyes to race the Tour Divide for a second time. My legs carried three months of solid training in Arizona, several scouting missions near my parents' place in British Columbia, premium gear, and the advantage of veteran knowledge. Unfortunately, a top result was not in the cards.

Setting out from a motel in Columbia Falls, Montana, at 4:30 a.m. on Day 3, I cringed in agony while trying to pedal up even the slightest of paved inclines. Pushing a record pace through the Canadian section had caused grinding knee injury. The pain forced me to walk up each successive climb, still 3000 km to go.

Two months later, the third chapter of our supported tour saw major forest fire reroutes around the Whitefish Divide in Montana. Riding with a Buff over my mouth at the U.S. border, thick smoke in the air around Lake Koocanusa, I felt the liability noose tightening. "This is the last time we're going to run this," I finally admitted, during a post-ride debrief at the Whitefish Bike Retreat. Fortunately the support for that decision encouraged me to acknowledge a valuable insight.

My crew and I had come to learn how new bikepackers think and operate in the backcountry. What are the hesitations of Floridian flatlander? How about a client from humid South Carolina? A prudent 60-year-old versus a headstrong 20-something? Someone who has been mountain biking for only a short time? Has never ridden lengthy back-to-back days? Or has limited camping experience? Writing a guidebook emerged as a way to parlay the knowledge bikepackers need to complete lengthy trips.

In March 2016 Sarah and I, now engaged and freelance business partners with Hammer Nutrition Canada, chose to move back across the country to Canmore, Alberta. We wanted to immerse ourselves full time in a mountain culture we had come to know and love on the tour. Subsequently, my focus for route research turned to the Canadian Rockies.

What happened next was an unexpected twist.

As part of my initial outline, I was tasked by Rocky Mountain Books with creating a list of relevant cycling resources: other guidebooks, maps, blogs, anything. Unfortunately, very little existed in the realm of off-road, ultralight adventures. Most links dealt with asphalt touring, utilizing heavy panniers loaded with everything but the kitchen sink. Additionally, anything that was mountain bike specific tended to cater only to the daytripper.

With the spur of New Year's resolutions, I quickly realized a more substantive opportunity. "To be a lifestyle leader and help build the Great North into a go-to destination," became the mission of my new, community-focused venture, Bikepack Canada (established January 2016). The mountain stoke now includes a podcast, an annual summit in Canmore, a growing list of overnighter group rides, tips being shared through our social channels, and ultimately, if I have done my job, a springboard for other pioneers in the community.

Welcome to our grand obsession.

BIKEPACKING 101

How does bikepacking differ from traditional road touring? What critical skills do you need to have before heading into the backcountry? These are the sorts of questions that will be addressed here. Just keep in mind, this is *not* an introduction to mountain biking.

It is therefore assumed that you have a least one year of off-road riding under your belt, are fit and resourceful, and have spent some time camping in the woods. Accordingly, the routes in this book are geared toward **Intermediate**, **Advanced** and **Expert** adventurers. Having this foundation will allow you to cut down on avoidable injuries and mechanical issues, open up more-technical terrain, have better recovery overnight, and ultimately create a more enjoyable experience for all involved. Furthermore, this will help you to understand your own abilities, so you can adjust the prescribed itineraries accordingly.

Bikepacking 101 is broken down into the following sections:

* What is Bikepacking?
* Developing a Solid Foundation
* Setting Out

What Is Bikepacking?

The term is a combination of "ultralight backpacking" and "multi-day mountain biking." Velcro packs that affix directly to the bike frame are a key piece of the equation. Many of us have chosen this equipment over traditional pannier racks due to concerns about metal fatigue (on bumpy tracks) and extra weight (on the long climbs). That said, one of my first organized overnighters was with a group of 20-somethings from Banff who had recently purchased junker bikes. They carried their camping gear in trash bags bungeed to rickety rear racks. And we had a blast!

The success of that outing was largely attributed to an adventurous DIY spirit rather than an adventurous spendy spree beforehand. Delving deeper into the bikepacking mantra:

- We prefer a backcountry path.
- We appreciate the opportunity to map unexplored routes.
- When speaking of technical difficulty, single-track trails are now added to a larger discussion of compounding days, foreign terrain, restock availability and established vs. wild camping.
- Like the backpacker, we appreciate the opportunity to connect with the natural world. We also champion the seven principles of Leave No Trace:
  1. Plan and prepare.
  2. Travel and camp on durable surfaces.
  3. Dispose of waste properly.
  4. Leave what you find.
  5. Minimize campfire impacts (be careful with fire).
  6. Respect wildlife.
  7. Be considerate of other visitors.
- Any racing is done for pure honour.
- We are fully self-supported.

Developing a Solid Foundation

"We have only ourselves to depend on," I often say in my talks. Just because we can press an SOS button does not mean that rescue is just around the corner. Please respect bikepacking as an inherently risky activity. Also, reading a guidebook does not make you an expert on the subject. There is much to be learned on the trail — more than I could ever include here.

BIKE HANDLING

Few bikepackers I know pay any attention to the exploits of adrenaline-seeking downhillers and/or fearless youth flying off dirt jumps. In fact, many of our routes can be accomplished by those with minimal technical riding ability. Being in the backcountry, however, we must be mindful of mitigating risk. Therefore:

- You should be comfortable riding single track, slippery roots, gravel, babyhead rocks, snow, mud and off-camber slopes. You should also know your limits on each.
- You should know (and have felt) the difference between a full-suspension bike and a hardtail one.
- You can balance your weight, front to back, side to side.
- You are comfortable with clipless pedals (if you are using them).

Any misgivings in your riding ability will be put to the test once your packs are loaded with anywhere from 2 to 22 kilos of gear.

PACKING THE RIGHT GEAR

Except for the Icefields Parkway (in winter), a hardtail 29er mountain bike is the gold standard for all routes listed in this guidebook. Ideally, pick a frame with a larger middle triangle. This will give you more packing potential. As for what is inside:

- Value function over flash.
- Think through how each piece of gear can be multi-purposed (for example, a jacket sleeve used as sling).
- Carry what you need, not what others suggest you take/not take.
- Carry backups, such as two forms of navigation, two forms of payment and so on.
- Weigh the pros and cons of battery-operated vs. dynamo-powered gadgets. (Solar has never really been a viable option in my experience.)
- Understand the layering principles of wicking, warming and weather resistance.
- Plan for all conditions (night riding, snow and so on).

See Appendix A for a sample ultralight packing list.

BIKE MAINTENANCE

Basic bike fixes often provide opportunities for our naivety to shine through (even for experienced riders). Set your ego aside and ask a local bike shop about registering for a clinic. It could make the difference between hiking out of the woods and being able to jimmy together a temporary fix, such as using a gel wrapper as a boot for a torn sidewall. While bikepacking, you should be able to:

- fix a flat tire in under ten minutes;
- know how to make your tires tubeless and use a CO_2 inflator;
- break a chain and put it back together using quick links;
- lube and clean your chain (What is dry lube? What is wet lube?);
- inflate your shocks when suspension is squishy;
- install a spoke and perform a basic true of a wheel;
- tighten and loosen all bolts and cables; and
- know the tools specific to your bike.

FITNESS

The routes in this guidebook were designed for an adult rider who can pedal upwards of 100 km/day. If you follow the prescribed route cues exactly, plan to be on your bike anywhere from five to 15 hours each day. Unknown variables of weather and trail conditions aside, ask yourself:

- What is my training plan? Is my goal to race or tour the route?

- Have I spent any time cross-training? (One of the most common injuries is Achilles tendonitis from engaging in hike-a-bike without having spent any time hiking in preparation.)
- Could I ride farther in an emergency?
- Am I strong enough to lift/push my bike over mountainous terrain?
- Are there any question marks associated with my health?

Be mindful of these considerations when planning your adventures. The prescribed itineraries for each route are ambitious, and it is highly recommended that you adjust your plans according to your own comfort level and abilities.

BODY CARE

You learn a lot about your body from injury and discomfort. They afford you the ability to differentiate between broken bones and sprains, understand how to stop critical bleeding, and ultimately make informed decisions when faced with the fight-or-flight adrenal response. Add to your checklist:

- How to keep warm. With cold being more of a concern than heatstroke in the Canadian Rockies, it is important to know how to minimize heat loss and warm yourself via fire, warm liquids, movement and layer management. You also need to understand how heat is transferred through conduction and convection (with the ground, air, stream crossings, snow and so on).
- Familiarity with a basic first aid kit (Band-Aids, antiseptic, tourniquet, triangular bandage) and the sense to customize for unique conditions.
- How to deal with repetitive injuries, the prime culprits being saddle sores, knee pain, numb hands, blisters and tight muscles.
- Knowing the difference between a minor rash and an infection.
- Appreciating the importance of basic hygiene. Wet wipes are your friend!
- Knowing what SPF rating of sunscreen you should be using.
- Having a good handle on any allergies and carrying the appropriate medication. An EpiPen is recommended, even if you haven't yet had an anaphylactic reaction.
- NSAIDS like Advil should be used sparingly. Get to the root of the problem.
- Knowing how to alleviate cramps and other muscle tightness with massage, stretching, hydration and increased electrolyte intake.

NUTRITION

You probably already have a good handle on what you like to eat while riding. Now also understand your body has enough fat to fuel itself across the country and back. Seriously! The key to active/ultra endurance nutrition is knowing how to stoke your internal energy reserves, not try to replace x calories burned with x calories consumed. It is physically impossible. Knowing this:

- Leave your picky eating habits at the door. Backcountry lodges and restaurants may not be able to accommodate all restrictions.
- Budget your calorie needs (200–400/hour is ideal)
- Understand the difference between simple sugar products, complex carbohydrates, protein and fats as fuel sources. You will likely pull from all of those.
- Consider your meal options. Are you stopping to cook? Banking on restaurants? On convenience store items? Each has its pros and cons as far as satiation, weight, cost and preparation time.
- Gain experience using iodine tablets and at least one other water-purification method.
- Understand what "bonking" means and how to kickstart your blood sugar.

NAVIGATION

Route cues sometimes fluctuate with the seasons: a flowing river runs dry during a summer drought, a track is obscured by winter deadfall, a backcountry cabin is sadly burned to the ground by ignorant campers. As such, carrying a GPS device is 100 per cent necessary.

- Know how to read your GPS device: breadcrumb track, contour lines, reliable drainages, intersecting roads, and service intersections.
- Know how to upload and manipulate GPX files and basemaps.
- Be comfortable asking for assistance from other backcountry users.
- Know how to read the physical terrain ahead: water generally flows through a valley bottom; a ridgeline helps you spot services ahead; and so on.

GPX files and updated addenda can be found at bikepack.ca/routes.

CAMPING

Both wild and established camping options are detailed for each route in this book. Make sure you:

- test various types of shelters, including a bivouac (bivi sack), tent and/ or tarp;
- are comfortable with improvised shelters such as an outhouse or tree well;
- know what temperature your sleeping bag should be rated for;
- know if you need a foam or air mattress to rest comfortably;
- can start a fire in a pinch, using matches or a lighter;

- know how to set up a bear hang for food and other smelly items; and
- follow the principles of Leave No Trace.

SEARCH AND RESCUE

Purchasing a national park pass ensures legal entry and will cover the cost of emergency rescue within the boundaries of Banff, Jasper, Kootenay and Waterton National Parks. Having a park pass will not cover emergency rescue fees if you are in a provincial park or on public land. And since none of the routes outlined in this book stay within one set of boundaries, you will want to come up with a comprehensive plan in the event of an emergency.

- Sign up for GEOS extraction coverage through either your SPOT or DeLorme satellite tracker. This is worldwide rescue coverage, good for two occurrences with a max support of US$50,000. Note that this covers *extraction only*. From GEOS: "This is not an insurance plan, travel insurance policy or a healthcare plan, and therefore GEOS will not reimburse members for expenses they incur on their own." A yearly plan starts at only US$17.95/year.
- If you have a healthcare card (each province issues its own), the Canada Health Act covers all medically necessary care in a hospital. Ambulance treatment/transfer is extra (C$250–385 in Alberta plus non-resident fee) if you do not have extended coverage such as Blue Cross. Do a bit of homework to understand the reach of your plan(s).
- Not a Canadian resident? Our free benefits do not apply, unfortunately. To have insured hospital care, you will need to secure an international travel insurance policy before entering the country.
- Engaging in a race may nullify the above policies. Again, do your research!

Setting Out

Now that you have developed a solid foundation, refocus your energy on better understanding each region of travel ahead of you. What are the connecting roads? The topography? And where can I bail if I need to? Consider this guide-book a *starting* point and branch out from here.

Furthermore, before leaving, you should research the long-range weather forecast. A meteorologist is rarely right about that "one rainy day" forecast 14 days from now. But a week of predicted rain...well, play the odds. And in the mountains, rain can easily turn to snow, even in the middle of July. If I had to choose one timeframe in which to tackle any of these rides — excluding areas with closures — it would be mid-August.

Additional points to consider before setting out:

- Get your bike tuned up. Better yet, know how to do it yourself!
- Connect with MTB groups and mountain bike clubs located near the trails you will be riding, to get up-to-date intel on trail conditions.
- Review road and trail closures by park authorities.
- Check for any wildlife concerns. Bears come out of hibernation in the spring and will be on the hunt for berries. Elk become quite aggressive during their fall rut.
- Book all your campsites and/or hostels in advance.
- Know your restock options and have cash on hand (in case of a power failure).
- Check water tables to get a sense of H_2O availability and possible flooding.
- If you are driving in, confirm where to park your car. You will find that many hotels accommodate extended parking if you stay at least one night. Starting at a hotel also gives you a good opportunity to assemble your gear in comfortable surroundings.
- Make sure your travel, extraction and health insurance plans are in place.
- Leave a detailed plan with family, including a link to your satellite tracking page.
- Head out on a test run to make sure all your gear is secured properly.

And, as always, please feel free to reach out to Bikepack Canada for further advice. Here we go!

INTERMEDIATE ROUTES

Are you newer to mountain biking and riding technical terrain?

Have you only camped at established, front-country campsites?

Are you new to multi-day touring?

Start here.

1. FRONT RANGE

START Hinton, Alberta

FINISH Canmore, Alberta

WHO SHOULD RIDE? A good off-road initiation for those who are newer to the fat-tire scene. Get your feet wet with an ample selection of straightforward gravel grinding.

DISTANCE 496 km

ELEVATION GAIN +6346 m / -6049 m

SUGGESTED NUMBER OF DAYS 4

About the Route

Venturing south along the Forestry Trunk Road in Alberta, you are immediately thrust into a rolling multi-use corridor for logging and mining industries and off-highway vehicle enthusiasts. Much of the inspiration for the Front Range trip comes from the original Alberta Rockies 700 event route, which continued another 227 km south to Coleman, Alberta. The route now consists of a new, looped track starting and ending in Canmore, Alberta (see Appendix D for full details).

Novice bikepackers will appreciate the availability of established campsites, non-technical riding along wide gravel roads, and ease of navigation. That said, do not underestimate the amount of climbing in these foothills! The Front Range rivals most traditional mountain passages.

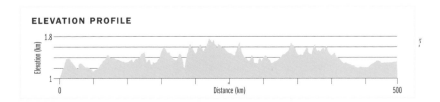

ELEVATION PROFILE

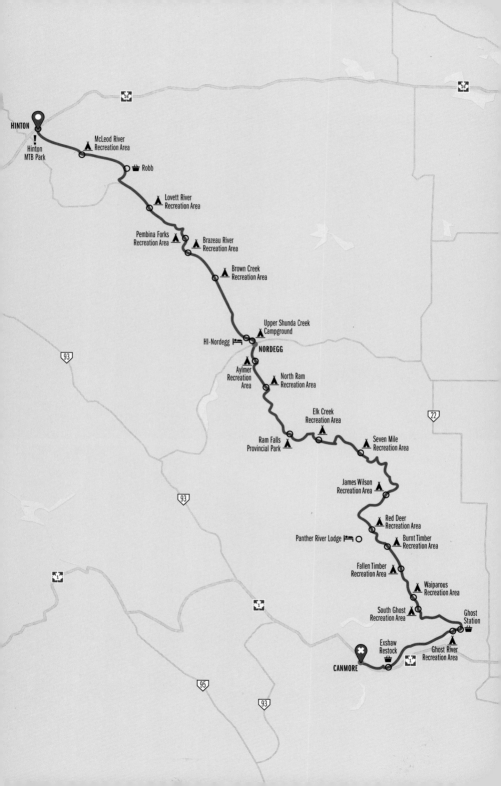

PHOTO: JEFF BARTLETT

Best time to go   A Sunday departure is recommended, to benefit from reduced logging and oil/gas traffic between Hinton and Nordegg. Campsites are generally open between May 1 and September 15. Mind you, this route travels almost entirely through Public Land Use Zones (more information at alberta.ca/public-land-use-zones.aspx). You can camp anywhere outside the leased operations, Stoney Nakoda land and Bow Valley Provincial Park. Essentially anywhere up until asphalt begins on Day 4.

Getting to Hinton   Edmonton is the closest international airport. Hinton is 286 km west of the city centre along the Yellowhead (Highway 16). The airport is an additional 30 km south of the city centre. Sundog Tours (sundogtours.com) can shuttle you directly from the airport to Hinton for $69 plus $30 for your bike, which must be boxed and booked in advance. If you live in Edmonton, you can catch the shuttle from West Edmonton Mall for $10 less.

Hitchhiking advisory   Commercial service trucks that frequent the route are technically not allowed to pick up hitchhikers. Should you get into a pinch, see if a truck driver would call ahead for help. All of them carry CB radios by law.

Transport back from Canmore   In the summer months, Brewster Express (www.banffjaspercollection.com/brewster-express) provides service from Canmore to Jasper. From there you can take a Sundog Tours shuttle back to Edmonton. See above.

Day 1: Hinton to Pembina Forks (99 km)

"Are you serious? These are the kind of hills we're going to be climbing?!" Sarah exclaimed as we hit the first stretch of rolling gravel. The former casual triathlete was about to get her first taste of bikepacking. It was the early morning of June 10, 2016. Our honeymoon.

HINTON RECOMMENDATIONS

Hinton is a busy commercial junction for those headed west to Jasper, north to Alaska or south down the Forestry Trunk Road. All services are centralized along the Yellowhead Highway. Learn more at hinton.ca.

Got an extra day?   Check out the Hinton Mountain Bike Park. 37 acres of designated trails, plus a skills area (bikehinton.com). Located 1.8 km south along the route.

Java fix The Old Grind (theoldgrind.ca) is adjacent to the visitor centre and is open 8:00 a.m. to 6:00 p.m., Monday to Saturday. Homemade food and live music.

Sleep on the cheap Hinton Centre Campground is conveniently located and is often used by out-of-town mountain bikers. Phone 780-865-0876. Alternatively, the Twin Pine Motel is one of the most economical in town. We stayed there in preparation for our honeymoon ride and the Alberta Rockies 700.

Stock up Freson Bros., located in a mall along Carmichael Lane, is part of a regionally owned chain of grocery stores. Open 7:00 a.m. to 11:00 p.m., daily. It is easy walking distance to the Twin Pine.

Tune up Vicious Cycle (viciouscanada.com) is on Park Street across from the start location. Open 10:00 a.m. to 6:00 p.m. most days. They close at 8:00 on Fridays. Vicious is the only bike shop in town.

0 km	Start at the Hinton Visitor Centre on Gregg Avenue. Open Monday to Friday, 9:00 a.m. to 7:00 p.m. Take an immediate right on Park Street, left on Pembina Avenue, then right on Switzer Drive, heading uphill.
1 km	Turn right on Robb Road. The paved road turns to gravel at the next intersection.
1.8 km	Hinton Mountain Bike Park on your right.
4.8 km	Take left fork onto Range Road 505A. There are several gravel and paved offshoots along the route from here on out. Keep straight unless directed otherwise.
26 km	Take left fork, heading downhill. Cross the McLeod River. The first of several established campsites is located here.
42.3 km	Keep right at fork for Priest Creek Road.
47.9 km	Turn right on paved Highway 47. Straight continues into the hamlet of Robb.
55.5 km	Highway 47 curves south at the nearly abandoned mining area of Coalspur.

57 km	Highway 40 comes in from the right. You are now on the Forestry Trunk Road. Coal Valley Mine runs parallel for the next several kilometres.
74.3 km	Road returns to gravel just past mine entrance.
99 km	Pembina Forks Campground ahead at the intersection of the Pembina and Elk rivers. $11/night plus $12 reservation fee. Water pump, pit toilets, and firewood available. Book in advance at albertaparks.ca.

Day 2: Pembina Forks to Ram Falls (132 km)

When I raced the inaugural Alberta Rockies 700 in 2016, less than two weeks after the "Honeymoon Scout," I purposely stocked up on enough food, and then some, to last me from Hinton to Canmore (roughly 9600 calories, 400 calories/hour). This calculated move allowed me to gain at least 30 minutes on riders who had no choice but to head off the route to restock at Nordegg — all did.

0 km	Continue south on the Forestry Trunk Road. The next set of services are at Nordegg, 72 km ahead.
1 km	Turn right at the fork for Elk River Road.
8 km	Brazeau Creek camping area on your right.
28.7 km	Brown Creek camping area on your right.
40 km	Cross the Brownstone River.
65.7 km	Turn left on unsigned OHV track across Shunda Creek meadow. Track connects to Shunda Creek Road.
67.8 km	HI Nordegg is on your right, open year-round. Upper Shunda Creek Campground is just ahead on your left.
70.7 km	Cross Highway 11 and follow an unsigned trail straight. It will curve left and connect with Stuart Street. Enter the hamlet of Nordegg.

Nordegg Recommendations

Nordegg caters to hunters and backcountry recreationists. All services are located within a few blocks. Learn more at nordeggliving.ca.

Foood! Aim for an early lunch or late breakfast at the Miners' Cafe (open daily, 9:00 a.m. to 6:00 p.m.). Make sure you take a quick tour of the attached museum after your meal. Take some time to digest before hitting the North Saskatchewan River valley.

Need to bail? Highway 11 is a main thoroughfare through central Alberta.

Restock Shell and Nordegg Lodge General Store and FasGas both have convenience items and propane for purchase. Both are generally open 6:00 a.m. to 10:00 p.m., daily.

Sleep on the cheap HI Nordegg is your most economical indoor option. Amenities include a hot tub, a hose to wash your bike, private rooms and small food items for purchase. Book in advance at hihostels.ca/en/destinations/alberta/hi-nordegg.

72 km	Turn right down an unsigned road, then continue along a dirt track. This scenic detour is part of Nordegg's new trail plan, approved in 2016 (if the trail is overgown or difficult to locate, retrace your path back to Highway 11, turn left and then take a left onto the Forestry Trunk Road).
74.6 km	Turn left on the Forestry Trunk Road and begin climbing for 2 km. An 8-km winding descent follows.
84 km	Cross a bridge over the North Saskatchewan River. Aylmer Camping area will be on your left. Begin a similar ascent out of the valley.
100.4 km	North Ram camping area.
131 km	The Alberta Forest Service's Ram Falls airstrip is on your right. Mostly abandoned, now only used by recreationists. One of a handful along the route.

Turn left into Ram Falls Provincial Park/Ram Falls Campground. $26/night plus a reservation fee ($12). Water pump and pit toilets. Firewood possibly for sale. Picture opportunity at Ram Falls lookout. One of the most picturesque campsites on the route. Book in advance at albertaparks.ca.

Day 3: Ram Falls to Burnt Timber (138 km)

During my first solo scout (before our honeymoon), I encountered a terrible bout of freezing rain and had to divert off the route to Sundre at the 120-km mark. Next, on the Alberta Rockies 700, my rear derailleur cable blew apart at almost the exact same location (forcing me to ride through the night with only one gear). If you should find yourself in a similar Red Deer River valley predicament, I encourage you to embrace the milkshake detour (see below).

0 km Continue south on the Forestry Trunk Road and cross the Ram River.

17.9 km Elk Creek camping area. The creek runs parallel until you begin climbing the range ahead. Make sure to treat your water: there are cattle in the area.

26 km Begin the challenging climb out of the valley.

31.4 km Keep straight at the Highway 752 turnoff. The town of Rocky Mountain House is 62 km off route. All services.

46.2 km Seven Mile camping area.

58.4 km Turn right on Highway 734 South. Straight continues 39 km to the village of Caroline. Limited services.

60 km Cross the Clearwater River.

88.3 km James Wilson camping area on your right.

120 km Keep straight at the turnoff for Township Road 312B. Sundre is 55 km off route. All services.

122 km Red Deer River North camping area. Cross the Red Deer River soon after. The former Mountain Aire Lodge is just ahead on your right.

MOUNTAIN AIRE LODGE (NOW CLOSED)

But if you are feeling burnt out, head 5 km off route to The Lodge at Panther River (pantherriver.com) or Sunset Guiding and Outfitting (sunsetguiding.com). The latter has food, accommodation and showers — and milkshakes!

124.2 km	Red Deer River South camping area (group sites).
138 km	Burnt Timber Campground on your right. $35/night plus $12 reservation fee. Water pump, pit toilets and firewood available. Book in advance at albertaparks.ca.

Day 4: Burnt Timber to Canmore (127 km)

Your route today becomes progressively easier as you slowly descend out of the gravel foothills and connect with front-country pavement. Embrace the lengthy asphalt entrance into the Bow Valley! It is a favourite amongst local road cyclists, although it can be windy in this direction.

0 km	Continue south on the Forestry Trunk Road.
13.7 km	Hunter Valley camping area.
30 km	Cross Waiparous Creek. There's a campground on the other side.
39 km	Asphalt begins, and the remaining 88 km to Canmore is paved.
41.4 km	Road curves left. Please do not take what appears to be a significant map shortcut along Richards Road (continuing straight to the 1A). Permission must be granted in advance by the Stoney Nakoda Nation. Year one of the AR700 went this direction. Subsequent years followed the route you are on.
48 km	Waiparous village. No services.
52 km	Village of Benchlands. Ghost River Emergency Service Centre alongside road.
65.6 km	Turn right at the intersection for Highway 1A/Bow Valley Trail. Nice asphalt but little to no shoulder for the next 36 km. Be mindful of traffic always. Travel in the early or late hours is not recommended.

GHOST STATION

The Ghost Station convenience store and campground (ghoststation.ca) is located 1 km ahead. Open Monday to Friday 8:00 a.m. to 9:00 p.m. Saturday to Sunday from 9:00 a.m. to 9:00 p.m.

69.6 km	Cross a bridge over the Ghost Reservoir. Recreation area and camping on the opposite side. Consider stopping here if it is getting late in the day. $26/night plus $12 reservation fee. Fire pits, pit toilets and a water pump. Book in advance at albertaparks.ca.

| 80 km | Enter unsigned Stoney Nakoda First Nations land. Please be respectful of the original people of the mountains. No wild camping for the next 22 km. |

| 80.6 km | Continue straight past the turnoff for unsigned Alberta 133x. A green bridge can be seen down the hill. It crosses the Bow River. |

MORLEY

The Stoney settlement of Morley is 1 km off route. Turn left, then left again after the bridge if you need to restock. There is a Subway restaurant and a convenience store here.

| 102 km | Enter unsigned Bow Valley Provincial Park. Mt. Yamnuska is on your right. The name comes from the Stoney word *yamnathka,* which refers to the mountain's flat face. |

| 109 km | Hamlet of Exshaw. Lafarge limestone mining operations ahead on the right. The company is the lifeblood of the community and is considered one of the most innovative cement plants in the world. |

HEART MOUNTAIN

If the westerly winds have got you at a standstill, stop for a break at Heart Mountain convenience store and café (heartmountainstore.com), open Monday to Friday 6:00 a.m. to 9:00 p.m. Saturday 7:00 a.m. to 9:00 p.m. and Sunday 7:00 a.m. to 8:00 p.m. The location is named after the heart-shaped mountain that it overlooks to the south.

| 110 km | Lac des Arcs on your left. |

| 122.4 km | Pass Indian Flats Road, the turnoff for the Alpine Club of Canada clubhouse (recommended stay). |

| 123.5 km | Cross under the Trans-Canada Highway and enter Canmore. Continue straight at a roundabout in 1.5 km. |

| 125.5 km | Turn left at an intersection for Railway Avenue. |

| 126 km | Turn left at an intersection for 8 Street (main street), then left again in a few blocks at 7 Avenue. |
| 127 km | Finish at the Canmore Civic Centre, 902 7 Avenue. |

CANMORE RECOMMENDATIONS

Bike shop & java fix Get your bike boxed up at the Bicycle Cafe (bicyclecafe.com), just a few doors down from the Grizzly Paw Pub on 8 Street. The cafe serves Stumptown Coffee from Portland, Oregon. A multipurpose stop for the espresso connoisseur. Rebound Cycle is another option. The friendly shop is very supportive of the bikepacking scene. See the Devil's Gap route for more information.

Foood! Grab a beer and homemade burger at the Grizzly Paw Pub (thegrizzlypaw.com), 622 8 Street. The brewery is just a few blocks down. Tours start at $17 and run Wednesday at 2:00 and 3:30 p.m. and Friday through Sunday at 1:00, 2:30 and 4:00 p.m. Best to book in advance.

Sleep on the cheap The Alpine Club of Canada Clubhouse (alpineclubofcanada.ca/web/ACCMember/Huts/Canmore_Clubhouse.aspx) is a world-class hostel with tremendous views of the Bow Valley. We used the acc as our base of operations for the supported Great Divide Mountain Bike Tour. It is a short taxi ride back to the clubhouse with your boxed bike. The Wapiti Campground is a little closer to downtown, but not nearly as nice. The Canmore Downtown Hostel is another option, having just opened in 2019.

* See the High Rockies and Devil's Gap routes for additional Canmore recommendations.

2. HIGH ROCKIES

START AND FINISH Banff, Alberta

WHO SHOULD RIDE? High Rockies entails several pitchy climbs alongside the Spray Lakes and the Rundle Mountain Range. Riders will appreciate the proximity to front-country services as they test more-technical, mtb-specific trails.

DISTANCE 182 km

ELEVATION GAIN 3302 m

SUGGESTED NUMBER OF DAYS 3

About the Route

Endeavour along a solid mix of classic and contemporary trails in and around Banff, Canada's first national park.

The prescribed circuit incorporates parts of the updated prologue of the Great Divide Mountain Bike Route (Banff townsite to Peter Lougheed Provincial Park), along the newly completed High Rockies Trail — a $3-million, 80-km extension of The Great Trail (also known as the Trans Canada Trail). The trail is well designed but challenging on a loaded bike, so plan your itinerary with additional days if in doubt.

Day 2 travels back north along the opposite side of the Kananaskis Range, cutting right through the heart of tourist country on trails above Highway 40. Stretching from the Trans-Canada Highway to Highwood Pass, this region is a popular launching point for horseback riders, golfers, hikers and skiers.

ELEVATION PROFILE

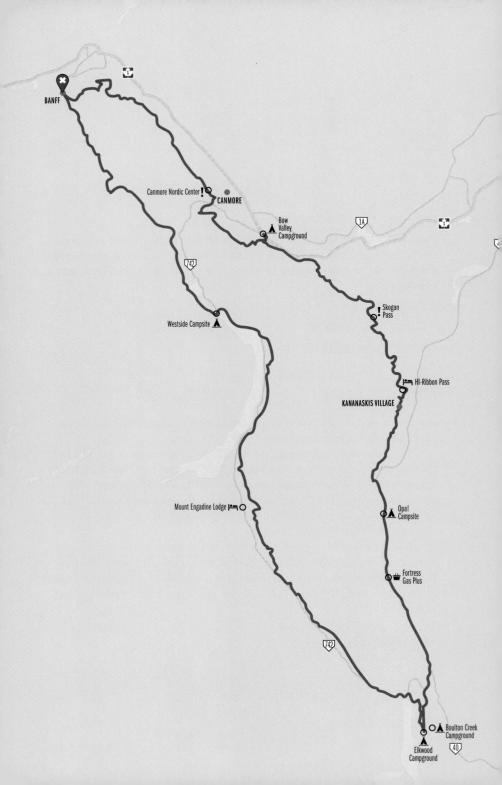

PHOTO: JEFF BARTLETT.

The final stretch climbs up and over Skogan Pass to Canmore's popular Highline Trail and the underutilized (and more technical) Rundle Riverside Trail. If you hiked any of the previous sections, expect to be off your bike some more.

Animal advisories   It is important to review animal advisories for Banff, Spray Lakes, Peter Lougheed Park and the Canmore Nordic Centre. You will be riding through the Yellowstone to Yukon wildlife corridor. Carrying bear spray is *essential*. Be cautious around bull elk during rutting season (autumn). Though rarely sighted, wolves and cougars also live here.

Getting to Banff   Calgary is the nearest international airport, located 145 km (1.5 hours west). There are several shuttle options that service the Bow Valley. Expect to pay roughly $60 for a one-way ticket.

When to go   There is only one seasonal closure. The golf course road (just outside Banff, Day 3) is closed from November to May.

Day 1: Banff to Elkwood (88 km)

Banff is hallowed ground for bikepackers around the world. The YWCA is the start location for our crown-jewel event, the Tour Divide. This annual unsanctioned race begins around 8:00 a.m. on the second Friday in June. Expect to see nearly 200 riders toeing the line.

Your track heads south through the Spray River valley. The iconic slant of the Rundle Mountain Range overlooks the first 30 km on your left, with Sulphur Mountain initially on your right. My suggestion to racers and touring cyclists alike is to temper your effort. Adrenalin can easily mask signs of the lactic acid that will no doubt accumulate on the gradual ascent to Goat Pond (above Canmore).

The route levels as you connect with the High Rockies just before the Spray Lakes reservoir. Once you cross the dusty Smith-Dorrien, the trail climbs up to a rolling bench that will be challenging for riders with heavier loads. There is a good selection of exits back down to the road, if needed.

BANFF RECOMMENDATIONS

This full-service destination was formed around the "discovery" of mineral springs along the Canadian Pacific Railway in 1859 (local Indigenous people had long known about these waters). The natural attraction inspired the first incarnation of the national park (originally 26 km²) in 1885, followed by the construction of the Banff Springs (now Fairmont) Hotel in 1887. Learn more at banff.ca.

Forget a layer?   Patagonia, at the south end of Main Street, is very supportive of the bikepacking scene. They have outfitted many a rider at the last minute. Open 10:00 a.m. to 8:00 p.m. Monday to Saturday; 10:00 a.m. to 6:00 p.m. on Sunday.

Java fix   Those in search of a top-notch cup of coffee will appreciate the Whitebark Cafe (whitebarkcafe.com) at 401 Banff Avenue, open 6:30 a.m. to 6:00 p.m. daily.

Sleep on the cheap   To really soak in the Divide experience, check out the YWCA hostel/hotel, ywcabanff.ca/hotel). A shared dorm room is inexpensive. The nearest campsites are atop Tunnel Mountain. Plenty of panoramic views and removed from the hustle and bustle of town, but a pretty challenging climb with a fully loaded pack and groceries in hand. More info at pc.gc.ca/en/pn-np/ab/banff/activ/camping.aspx.

Stock up   Head on over to the IGA at 318 Marten Street, open 8:00 a.m. to 11:00 p.m. daily.

Tune up   There are two bike/ski shops in Banff, both within walking distance of each other on Bear Street. Snowtips-Backtrax (snowtips-bactrax.com) is open 7:00 a.m. to 9:00 p.m. daily. Stop here if you need to rent any camping equipment for the journey. At the south end of Bear, Soul Ski & Bike (soulskiandbike.com) is open 10:00 a.m. to 8:00 p.m. daily. Owner Jason Kucey has previously reached out to Tour Divide riders who need somewhere to ship their bikes.

Additional Banff recommendations can be found on the Icefields Parkway (in winter) route.

0 km	Begin at the YWCA. The hostel / long-term housing is located at the south end of town, just across the historic Bow River Bridge (constructed in 1927). Head south along Spray Avenue.
1 km	Fairmont Banff Springs hotel on your right. At the far end of the parking lot, continue straight to the Spray River trailhead. If racing the Tour Divide, expect a neutral rollout over the next 18 km.

7 km	At a clearing with a wooden shelter, stay straight on the main trail. The path heading left doubles back along the opposite side of the Spray River.
11 km	Turn left at signed junction for Canmore, heading downhill. Cross the Spray River bridge and begin a steep 200-m push up what is now Goat Creek Trail.
13.2 km	Cross Goat Creek and begin another steep 200-m climb. You may have to hike this section if not in an easy gear before the bridge.
19.3 km	Turn left, heading down the High Rockies Trail. Cross Goat Creek and enter a hydro corridor on the opposite side. You are now in Spray Valley Provincial Park.
29.2 km	Turn left and head across the Spray Lakes Dam road. Spray Lakes West Campground is straight ahead, 2.6 km off route. Fellow movie buffs will appreciate that Hollywood films like *The Revenant* and *The Edge* have utilized this area for rugged shoots.
29.8 km	Turn right, keeping on the trail along the lake.
33.1 km	Trail heads up across the gravel Smith-Dorrien Trail. Continue up hillside along the High Rockies. The rolling gradient remains relatively consistent for next 50.2 km.

35.1 km	Intersection with West Wind Trail. Possible exit back down to the Smith-Dorrien.
41.4 km	Intersection with Read's Tower Route. Possible exit.
50.5 km	Intersection with Buller Pass Trail. Possible exit.
55.7 km	Intersection with Rummel Lake Trail. Possible exit.

MOUNT ENGADINE LODGE

Mount Engadine Lodge is the only commercial service in Peter Lougheed Provincial Park. Afternoon tea is served from 2:00 to 5:00 p.m. daily at $22.50/person. $$$ rooms and yurts also available. Located at the bottom of Rummel Lake Trail. Learn more at mountengadine.com.

62.7 km	Intersection with Chester Lake Trail. Possible exit.
70.2 km	Intersection with Sawmill Loop parking area. Possible exit.
83.3 km	High Rockies drops down to the Smith-Dorrien. Continue straight across the Lower Kananaskis Lake dam. Keep an eye on your GPS as you navigate bike paths to Elkwood.
87.6 km	Turn right on Kananaskis Lakes Trail.
87.8 km	Elkwood Campground. $29/night plus $12 reservation fee. Book in advance at albertaparks.ca. Showers and payphones available.

BOULTON CREEK CAMPGROUND

Boulton Creek Campground is 3.7 km farther down Kananaskis Lakes Trail from Elkwood Campground. The camp store has basic convenience items.

Day 2: Elkwood to Bow Valley (60 km)

This was a major reroute after I learned from Alberta Parks that the West Side Road (my original return route around Spray Lakes) was being turned into a restricted wildlife corridor. You now venture north along the adjacent Kananaskis Valley to Skogan Pass. Not a bad consolation prize.

0 km	Continue north along paved Kananaskis Lakes Trail for 6 km.
6.2 km	Turn left on Highway 40. Right heads up Highwood Pass.

FORTRESS GAS PLUS

At 14.7 km, Fortress Gas Plus (fortressjunction.ca) is on your left. Open 8:00 a.m. to 10:00 p.m. in the summer. The online services page lets you know if the ice cream, hot dog and slush machines are working. They take convenience seriously!

20.3 km	Opa! Camping area on the left.
23.5 km	Turn right into Galatea Creek Provincial Recreation Area. Connect with Galatea Lakes Trail just ahead.
24.1 km	Fork right onto Terrace South Trail. Keep on this all the way to Kananaskis Village.
31.3 km	Cross Terrace Drive and keep straight through Kananaskis Village.

KANANASKIS VILLAGE

$$$ Pomeroy Kananaskis Mountain Lodge, restaurant, pub and Market Cafe are central. The cafe opens at 6:00 a.m. Closing hours may vary. They have convenience items, coffee, food and tourist trinkets.

31.8 km	Connect with paved Bill Milne Trail on opposite side of the village.
34 km	Turn right on Centennial Drive. Intersection for Ribbon Creek Road and HI Kananaskis Wilderness Hostel just ahead. Book in advance at hihostels.ca.
34.3 km	Turn left on Mount Allan Drive.
35.5 km	Turn right at parking lot for Nakiska Ski Area (day lodge closed for the season). This hill hosted the 1988 Winter Olympic alpine and mogul ski events. Continue up the back side of its maintenance area.

36.2 km	Turn left up Skogan Pass Trail. Keep a close eye on your GPS. Several intersecting ski trails and hiking paths on your route up the mountain.
44.9 km	Top out at an elevation of 2059 m. Begin weaving down a cutline.

VIEW

100 m before the summit, turn up the unmarked trail for a clear view back down the valley.

53.1 km	Bottom out at a T-junction. Turn right, through a parking lot and down George Biggy Sr. Road.
54.0 km	Cross a rustic wooden bridge over Pigeon Creek, then pick up a double track trail following a powerline that parallels the Trans-Canada Highway.
58.4 km	Enter a residential area. Slight right onto Stewart Creek Rise.
58.5 km	At a roundabout, take the first exit down Three Sisters Parkway.
59.0 km	Turn right on Three Sisters Boulevard and cross the Trans-Canada.
60.1 km	Bow River Campground. This site underwent major renovations in 2017 and now includes showers, toilets, water pump, electricity and firewood. $29/night plus $12 reservation fee. Book in advance at albertaparks.ca.

Day 3: Bow Valley to Banff (34 km)

A more technical final stretch along the High Rockies and Rundle Riverside Trail. Halfway, you have the opportunity to play around at the Canmore Nordic Centre, a legacy of the 1988 Calgary Winter Olympics. In addition to cross-country skiing and biathlon, the provincial park also hosts several internationally recognized mountain bike events. There is no cost for using the trails in summer, a network of over 100 km. Check out albertaparks.ca/canmore-nordic-centre.

0 km	Backtrack up Three Sisters Boulevard, past Three Sisters Parkway and all the way to the end of the road.

1.6 km Pick up the narrower Highline Trail heading up through the trees. Keep an eye on your GPS, as there are several intersecting paths ahead. Also watch for high meltwater flows, rock slides and so on. The "mine side" (shady south side) of the Bow Valley is the last to melt in spring/early summer.

2.7 km Cross a bridge over Three Sisters Creek. The trail kicks up after the next two junctions. Watch for local riders bombing down.

7.2 km Turn right down Highline West Connector.

8.3 km Turn left up Powerline Trail.

9.7 km Turn right down a track that will soon hug the east side of the Canmore reservoir. Great views down the Bow Valley.

11.9 km Turn left on paved Three Sisters Parkway, then right, into Canmore Nordic Centre Provincial Park in 300 m. At the day lodge, follow signage for Banff Avenue (heading west past the biathlon shooting area). Pay close attention to your GPS. There are many intersecting trails.

CANMORE NORDIC CENTRE

Energy to burn? Take on the 17.5-km 24 Hours of Adrenalin double/single-track loop. Ask for a $2 trail map at the day lodge (you might need it). Budget two hours to complete the circuit. Also, bear spray is highly recommended while riding at the Nordic Centre.

Restock Cornerstone Café (inside the day lodge) is open 9:00 a.m. to 5:00 p.m. year-round.

Tune up Trail Sports (trailsports.ab.ca) is an on-site rental business that may be able to help with minor repairs. They are open 9:00 a.m. to 8:00 p.m. Monday through Thursday and 9:00 a.m. to 6:00 p.m. Friday through Sunday. For a more substantial tune-up, or in an emergency, descend on the Three Sisters Parkway for another 4 km down into Canmore.

18.3 km	Connect onto Rundle Riverside Trail at the west end of the Nordic Centre trail system. The Bow River will come into view as you begin a rooty and more technical final push to Banff.
26.6 km	Turn right on the paved Banff Springs golf course road (a one-way loop).
32.5 km	The golf course clubhouse is on your right.
33.3 km	Cross a bridge over the Spray River and turn right. Start up Bow River Avenue. Bow Falls overlook in 200 m.
33.9 km	Turn right on Glen Avenue. Keep straight down a quiet backstreet.
34.5 km	Finish at the YWCA.

BANFF RECOMMENDATIONS

Foood! The Banff Ave. Brewing Company (banffavebrewingco.ca) is a great supporter of local events. The beer is made on site by Bear Hill Brewing. They also have a full menu of complementary recovery meal options. Poutine anyone?

Got an extra day?   Head over to the Cave and Basin National Historic Site for a tour of the mineral springs, then take on the 5.7-km climb up Sulphur Mountain (listed as "Sulphurfest" on Trailforks.com). Just be aware that you must ride the same way back down — the hiking trail and gondola do not allow bikes. Tremendous views from an elevation of 2300 m. Food and coffee are also available in the newly refurbished gondola building. The gondola is open 8:00 a.m. to 9:30 p.m. in the summer.

3. BEAVERFOOT

START AND FINISH   Golden, British Columbia

WHO SHOULD RIDE?   Beaverfoot is characterized by wide-open gravel roads through the valley of the Columbia and Beaverfoot Rivers. The main challenge will be navigating a few unsigned links. A beneficial GPS primer for more technically challenging routes ahead.

DISTANCE   389 km

ELEVATION GAIN   4847 m

SUGGESTED NUMBER OF DAYS   4

About the Route

The opening Trans-Canada Highway passage through the Kicking Horse valley has been undergoing a four-phase, $767-million twinning since 2006: 21 km of highway has been significantly levelled and widened (with a 2.5-m shoulder for cyclists). My original hope was to bypass the highway by circling up through Yoho National Park. Unfortunately, all possible connecting routes off the Blaeberry Forest Service Road have been flooded, are in disrepair and/or are restricted to hiking. That particular scout showed what can happen to a backcountry recreation area when forestry operations are no longer invested.

The afternoons of Days 1 and 2 are spent along the quiet, meandering banks of the Beaverfoot and Kootenay rivers. Take this opportunity to imagine a time when there was no gravel, just a confluence to navigate, a ridge to catch your bearings, and a life constructed through the tenacity of your own two hands.

ELEVATION PROFILE

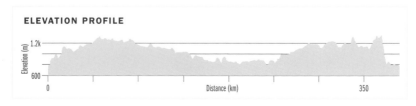

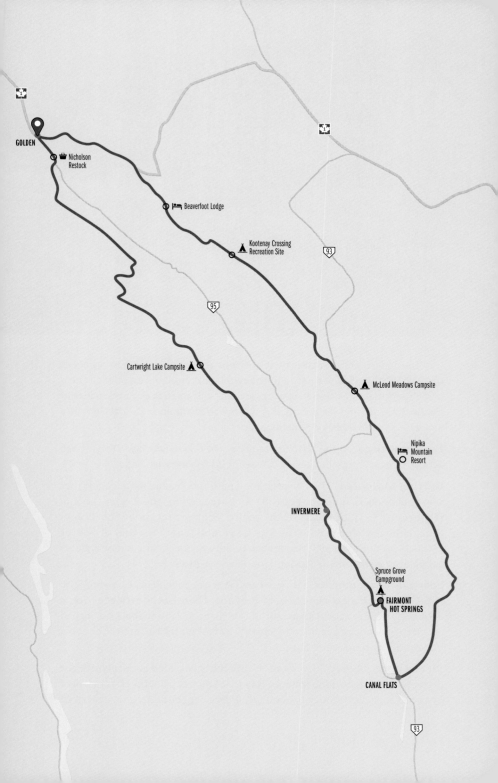

In the wake of that time of settlement and exploration, the adjacent Columbia River valley is now a tourism hotspot for boaters, golfers, hikers and hot-springers. Fortunately your passage back north is along the fringe of the Rocky Mountain Trench, up through hobby farms and extensive ranches along the remote Bugaboo benchlands.

Best time to go   June 15 to September 5, to take advantage of the listed campgrounds. They will likely be booked solid on long weekends.

Getting to Golden   The nearest international airport is Calgary. From there, Golden is three hours (281 km) west along the Trans-Canada Highway. The final phase of the major reconstruction of the Trans-Canada near Golden, scheduled to be completed by the end of winter 2023–24, may still be affecting traffic. Be sure to check for current updates at gov.bc.ca/gov/content/kicking-horse-canyon-project.

Possible developments   Howse Pass (at the north end of Blaeberry) into Banff National Park is a link to keep an eye on. There has been talk for over a decade of trying to extend a rail trail and/or Highway 11 from Red Deer up and over the Continental Divide into Golden. The first fur traders in the Columbia Valley traversed this very route.

Please note   A July 2019 scout of this route revealed some significant setbacks with parts of the track on Day 1. At kilometre 74, the water level of Symond Creek was too high to permit walking along the drainage as described below in the route cues (and as required in order to avoid crossing private land). Even more problematic, West Kootenay Trail, at kilometre 77, has been decommissioned and was obstructed by significant deadfall.

In light of these issues, an alternative option is to ride the route point-to-point, omitting most of Day 1. Riders could begin the route on Highway 93 South at kilometre 98.4 (or farther north on Highway 93 if one is not averse to riding on pavement). The remainder of the route is beautiful and worth the effort to find a viable detour.

Day 1: Golden to McLeod Meadows (106 km)

The first stretch of the Trans-Canada Highway here is still under construction (remnants of the old highway can be seen in the Kicking Horse River valley below). Keep an eye out for slow-moving vehicles and mountain sheep on the almost non-existent shoulder. You soon exit south into the more remote Beaverfoot Valley. There, look for hand-lettered signs teasing pizza at Beaverfoot Lodge. A good opportunity to double-check the batteries in your GPS unit, which will become important from 69 km onward.

GOLDEN RECOMMENDATIONS

All services are available ("Golden Rules"). Learn more at tourismgolden.com.

Got an extra day? Make sure to check out the vast network of cross-country and downhill mountain bike trails, all within a few kilometres of town, Kicking Horse Resort being a prime destination. The Golden Cycling Club (goldencyclingclub.com) has a trail app you can download.

Java fix With Golden being such a ski/bike/hike mecca, there are plenty of homegrown options for the dirtbag crew to choose from (there are more commercial options up along the Trans-Canada). Purcell Coffee has the best rating on TripAdvisor. They roast their own coffee too! Open 7:30 a.m. to 4:30 p.m. on Monday, Tuesday and Friday; 10:00 a.m. to 3:00 p.m. on Thursday; and 8:00 a.m. to 3:00 p.m. on the weekend.

Stock up The two grocery stores are Save-On-Foods and IGA. Both are open 8:00 a.m. to 9:00 p.m. daily.

Tune up Higher Ground Sports (highergroundsports.ca) is open Monday to Saturday 9:00 a.m. to 7:00 p.m. and 10:00 a.m. to 6:00 p.m. on Sunday. Derailed Sports (derailedsports.com) is another option in town, and more cycling-centric. They have similar hours.

0 km	Start from the Kicking Horse Chamber of Commerce at 500 10 Avenue North. Continue north out of town, following 10 Avenue / Highway 95, turning left up the overpass in 500 m.
1.5 km	Just before forking uphill (west) onto the Trans-Canada toward Banff, cut over to the Golden Hill bike path running alongside.
3 km	Golden Hill path intersects Golden View Road. Turn left in 200 m, heading onto the Trans-Canada Highway. Paved road for the next 23 km.
6 km	Begin a narrow and windy section out of town. Little to no shoulder, with impeding gravel and good possibility of encountering mountain sheep. Road conditions improve significantly at the last bend, in 3 km.
11 km	Cross the Kicking Horse River.
13.2 km	Rest stop with washrooms on your left. The pedestrian path you see snaking east through the valley unfortunately terminates just past the massive, 90-metre-high Park Bridge. Keep to the highway.
26.4 km	Turn right on Beaverfoot Road, which quickly turns to gravel. Heading down over the Kicking Horse River, watch for chalets and a guiding business on your right. Keep straight unless directed otherwise. Forestry road offshoots become more frequent as you head deeper into the valley.
40.5 km	Beaverfoot Lodge (beaverfootlodge.com) on your left. Wood-fired pizza and accommodations. Cabins are $$$. Tent camping and wagon rentals also available.
51.4 km	At a turnoff for Marion Lake, stay left on Beaverfoot Road. There's an abundance of wild camping opportunities in the area. You are on public land sandwiched between Yoho to the north and Kootenay National Park to the south and east.

60.8 km	Kootenay Crossing Recreation Site, where Marion Lake Road loops back to the Beaverfoot. Consider stopping here if it is getting dark. If you continue, pay attention to your GPS.
69.5 km	Look for a right turn at a yellow 42.5 marker. This is the most obvious route to continue on, as referenced in Doug Eastcott's wildly popular *Backcountry Biking in the Canadian Rockies* (Rocky Mountain Books, 2001, 2011). Unfortunately, you now intersect a small swath of private land and, within 3 km, a "Do Not Enter" gate. When I spoke with the kind, elderly owners, they told me they had never refused entry to riders who respect the property and do not camp near their rustic cabin (just past the gate on the left). For the sake of establishing a more sustainable route with GPS coordinates, please follow the new route listed below.
74 km	At Symond Creek, running perpendicular to Beaverfoot Road, hop off your bike and follow the drainage right (south). Turn left at the fork near the bottom, then hike up to the overgrown vehicle path ahead.
75.3 km	Continue southeast along Settlers Road. Last chance for wild camping before entering national park lands.

77 km	Path becomes West Kootenay Trail (and enters Kootenay National Park) at the boulders across the trail. Sign indicates 12.8 km to Kootenay Crossing.
88.8 km	At a signed junction, turn right, heading up toward Luxor Pass. In an emergency, keep left for 1 km to the Kootenay Crossing warden station (along Highway 93).
93 km	Keep left on Dolly Varden (you may not even notice the intersection for Luxor Pass, a narrow hiking trail heading up to the right). As you begin descending, keep in control of your speed. There is a bridge out toward the bottom — not so obvious to spot when looking through taller grass or in poor light.
98.4 km	Enter Crook's Meadow Group Camping (available for non-profit groups). Proceed to Highway 93. If the campsite gate is closed, lift your bike through the adjoining pedestrian gate. Turn right onto a smooth highway with good shoulder.
106.4 km	McLeod Meadows Campground on your left. There are 80 quiet sites along the wooded bank of the Kootenay River. $21.97/night at the self-register. Fire pits. Open mid-June to mid-September.

Day 2: McLeod Meadows to Fairmont Hot Springs (106 km)

Your day begins down a dusty bottleneck for logging trucks that services the Kootenay River valley. Have your Buff at the ready to cover your mouth and nose. The fine dust can be both blinding and hard on the lungs. The valley opens after the 20-km mark. Begin early so you can take in the hot springs (and cold pools) at Fairmont.

0 km	Continue south on Highway 93. Good shoulder.
7.3 km	Turn left on gravel Settlers Road. Be cautious of logging trucks (and the fine dust they kick up) for the next 12 km.
19.7 km	Junction for Nipika Mountain Resort (nipika.com), less than 1 km off route. $$$ log cabins available for rent. They also have a great network of cross-country trails. Just note that this is *not* a restock point. Keep right on Settlers Road through the Kootenay River valley.
52.8 km	Turn right onto Kootenay Forest Government Road. Good views of the Kootenay River along this stretch.

PHOTO: JEFF BARTLETT

75.5 km	Keep straight at junction for Nine Mile Forest Service Road.
79.4 km	J2 Ranch (j2ranch.com) is on the south side of the river valley. Begin small switchback up into the trees.
82.2 km	Keep right at a private road heading down to the Canfor mill. Begin descent.
84.3 km	Near the bottom, turn right on unsigned gravel road. Track runs parallel to the paved Grainger Road for the next kilometre. If in need of a restock, continue down into Canal Flats.

CANAL FLATS RECOMMENDATIONS

A timber town with a population of 668 (as of the 2016 census) that was hard hit by the closure of the Canfor mill in late 2015. Basic services, all within a few blocks of hitting asphalt.

Foood! and java fix Viibrant Earth Cafe (viibrantearth.ca) is open Wednesday through Sunday from 9:00 a.m. to 1:00 p.m.

Restock Canal Flats Family Foods is on Arbuckle Street. Open daily from 8:00 a.m. to 8:00 p.m.

Sleep on the cheap The Flats RV and Campground (theflatsrv.com). Rent out a vintage Boler or Airstream trailer for ~$100/night. Tenting is $27.50/night (including hot showers). Convenience store on site.

89.3 km	As the road curves uphill, turn left onto the unmarked Spirit Trail. Begin with a 2-km downhill. Keep an eye on your GPS through this section. Your path will weave in and out of Columbia Lake Provincial Park.
103.8 km	Reach paved Columbia River Road.

104.8 km Turn left on Fairmont Creek Road, then left again on Highway 93. Straight takes you Fairmont Hot Springs services.

FAIRMONT RECOMMENDATIONS (EVENING)

Rest those weary legs   Bring a swimsuit for yourself and a lock for your bike. Fairmont Hot Springs (fairmonthotsprings.com) is 3.6 km up from Spruce Grove Campground. Admission is $21 for adults ($26 July to September). There is also a free foot bath just a short hike up from the main pool. Please note that the natural source of the springs is roped off from public use.

Restock   Fairmont Mountainside Market is along Highway 93 on Fairmont Frontage Road. Open daily from 8:00 a.m. to 8:00 p.m.

| 105.5 km | Left into Spruce Grove Campground. Unserviced tent sites were $31–$33/night in 2019, cash or credit card. Amenities include showers, fire pits, WiFi, laundry and a camp store. Book in advance at fairmonthotsprings.com/rv-camping/spruce-grove-campground. Closer to the hot springs, there may also be camping available in the RV Resort, T1–10 loop. $32/night. The former has greater availability. |

Day 3: Fairmont Hot Springs to Cartwright Lake (82 km)

Take in the panoramic views as you ride north along Westside Road through the Rocky Mountain Trench (the western edge of the Rockies). Past the town of Invermere the route slowly ascends to the Bugaboo benchlands (part of the Purcell Mountains). In the many months of scouting, this was the only area where I encountered bears.

FAIRMONT RECOMMENDATIONS (MORNING)

Java fix   Valley Coffee Co. (facebook.com/ValleyCoffeeBC) is open 8:00 a.m. to 3:00 p.m. daily. Located on Fairmont Frontage Road next to Fairmont Mountainside Market.

0 km	Continue south on Highway 93.
2.3 km	Turn right on Westside Road. There are markers in the ditch for a Westside Legacy Trail (ourtrail.org). The 25-km, $8.7-million Fairmont Hot Springs to Invermere connector began construction in spring 2017 and as of spring 2020 was 90 per cent funded.
26.2 km	Westside Road turns into 13 Avenue on the outskirts of Invermere.
28.1 km	Turn right on 13 Street.
28.9 km	Turn left at T-junction for 7 Avenue (main street). Stores in the area are your last resupply opportunity for 140 km.

INVERMERE RECOMMENDATIONS

Invermere is the commercial hub for the Columbia Valley. Learn more at columbiavalley.com.

Java fix   Detour farther down the hill (after 30 km) to visit the headquarters of Kicking Horse Coffee (kickinghorsecoffee.com). In addition to producing one of Canada's favourite Fairtrade products, the business is also a great supporter of mountain culture events. The cafe is open Monday to Friday 7:00 a.m. to 5:00 p.m.; Saturday 8:00 a.m. to 5:00 p.m.; and Sunday 9:00 a.m. to 4:00 p.m.

Tune up   There are three bike shops in town, all within a few blocks: Bicycle Works (bicycleworks-bc.com), Elemental Cycle (elementalcycle.com) and Columbia Cycle & Ski (columbiacycle.ca).

30 km	Fork right on 3 Street (7 Avenue continues straight), then a quick left on Panorama Drive in 200 m. Enter a more industrial area.
32 km	Panorama Drive becomes Toby Creek Road, heading uphill. Just across Toby Creek bridge, turn right on Wilmer Road.
32.6 km	Kootenae House National Historic Site on the right. Established as a fur-trade hub and base of exploration for the Columbia Valley in 1807.
34.5 km	Enter the tiny community of Wilmer (no services). Turn right on Main Street. The gravel Westside Road begins at the north end of town. Keep straight unless otherwise directed.
39.8 km	Begin going up to the bench overlooking Horsethief Hideout (horsethiefhideout.com), a western-themed group facility with camping by donation. Call 250-347-6407 for availability. They have hot showers.
65.2 km	Farm on your left.
71.3 km	Turn left up unmarked Leadqueen Frances Road. Keep left at following fork.
76.4 km	Whary Lake on your right.
81 km	Cartwright Lake Recreation Site backcountry camping area on your right. Easy access. If occupied, continue.

82 km Path curves around to the north side of the lake and Recreation Site. Quieter sites here. No reservation or fee required.

Day 4: Cartwright Lake to Golden (95 km)

Dig deeper into the Bugaboo benchlands, the most remote section of the entire route.

0 km Head back to Leadqueen Frances Road and turn right (north).

6.2 km Turn left on Bugaboo Creek Road.

8.5 km Cross Bugaboo Creek.

11 km Turn right up unsigned Bobbie Burns Forest Service Road.

30.5 km Cross Bobbie Burns Creek and begin climbing.

32.5 km Turn right up Spillimacheen Forest Service Road. Top out in 2 km.

40.4 km Cross the Spillimacheen River. Take next right and begin the steep push up Crestbrook Mainline.

43 km Top out and begin a winding descent down Crestbrook Road.

PHOTO: JEFF BARTLETT

50 km	Turn left on an unsigned road. Begin the Parson to Nicholson OHV trail. Described as a "wide logging road with many spurs and areas to explore. Many grown-over areas." Keep a close eye on your GPS.
79 km	Turn right on the more established Nicholson Creek Road.
84.7 km	Cross Canyon Creek and enter the Columbia River Basin.
85.4 km	Fork right on Canyon Creek Road.
86.9 km	Cross the Columbia River and enter the small community of Nicholson. Turn left on Nicholson Road. RaceTrac Gas (and convenience store) is just ahead.
88.1 km	Turn left on Highway 95. There is a good shoulder.
93.9 km	Continue straight through downtown Golden.

GOLDEN RECOMMENDATIONS

Foood! The Wolf's Den (thewolfsdengolden.ca) is a top-rated local pub on TripAdvisor. Open Monday to Thursday 4:00 p.m. to 10:00 p.m. and Friday to Sunday 4:00 p.m. to 11:00 p.m. Tons of greasy burger options, made fresh every day.

Souvenir brew Grab a Belgian-inspired growler from Whitetooth Brewing Company (est. 2016), located at 623 8 Avenue North (whitetoothbrewing.com). Open 2:00 p.m. to 10:00 p.m. every day but Tuesday.

95 km	Finish at the Chamber of Commerce.

II.

ADVANCED ROUTES

---

*Are you comfortable on
technical mountain bike terrain?*

*Could you pull off the trail
and camp anywhere?*

*Ready to challenge
more remote climbs?*

Giddy up!

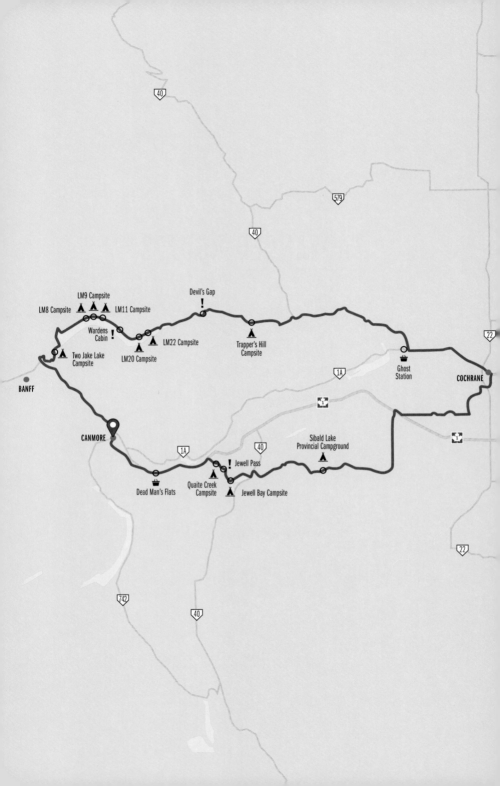

4. DEVIL'S GAP

START AND FINISH Canmore, Alberta

WHO SHOULD RIDE? A progression into more advanced navigation, technical riding, hike-a-bike and backcountry camping. In terms of access to services, it is recommended that you complete the High Rockies route before attempting this more remote track.

DISTANCE 215 km

ELEVATION GAIN 2399 m

SUGGESTED NUMBER OF DAYS 3

About the Route

Banff National Park has started to see upwards of 4 million visitors per year. The Trans-Canada Highway, the paved Legacy Trail, Highway 93, Bow Valley Parkway and Icefields Parkway are primary entry points for vehicles and road-touring cyclists. As for off-road veins, your options have traditionally been limited to two: Goat Creek and Rundle Riverside Trail — which we have explored.

A third, lesser known entry does exist, however. It is the Devil's Gap (named for Devil's Head mountain) between Lake Minnewanka, the largest body of water in the Canadian Rockies, and the Ghost River valley, a provincially regulated public land use zone along the Front Range. There are three good reasons why few mountain bikers have navigated this back entrance.

ELEVATION PROFILE

1. It cannot easily be completed in a day.
2. There is potential for more than 10 km of hike-a-bike.
3. No discernible trail exists through the Gap.

The bikepacking bold should be captivated by this challenge.

Banff's first tourist "In July 1841, a pack train of 45 horses and 25 men entered the Rocky Mountains through Devil's Gap at the eastern end of Lake Minnewanka. Sir George Simpson, governor of the Hudson's Bay Company, was in the midst of an around-the-world tour, and this stage of the adventure entailed crossing the mountains by a route never before followed by non-Aboriginal travellers." (From Emerson Sanford and Janice Sanford Beck, *Life of the Trail 5: Historical Hikes around Mount Assiniboine and in Kananaskis Country.*)

Best window to go The Lake Minnewanka seasonal trail is *closed to cyclists* from July 10 to September 15, due to bears feeding on berries along the south-facing slope. You will be slapped with a substantial fine if you go in anyway, and you can be tracked by animal camera. September 16 to mid-October is the ideal window. Early spring and summer are busy with tourist traffic.

Getting to Canmore Calgary is the international airport, located 122 km (1.25 hours) west. There are several shuttles that service the Bow Valley, including the Banff Airporter. Expect to pay roughly $70 for a one-way ticket.

Day 1: Canmore to Barrier Lake (30 km)

Navigation from Canmore to the trail up Jewell Pass is bound to see some big changes soon. At this writing, completion of The Great Trail (also known as the Trans Canada Trail) link is competing with plans to expand Three Sisters Mountain Village through the Bow Valley wildlife corridor (to Dead Man's Flats). Wherever the route settles, the climb up and over to Barrier Lake is and will remain a favourite among day hikers and backcountry cyclists.

CANMORE RECOMMENDATIONS

Java fix The best mountain view can be found at Beamer's (beamerscoffee.ca) on 7 Avenue, open 6:00 a.m. to 7:00 p.m. daily. Eclipse Coffee Roasters (eclipsecoffeeroasters.com) on Main Street is a favourite with coffee afficionados, open 8:00 a.m. to 5:00 p.m. daily.

Stock up   Safeway and Save-On-Foods are located within walking distance on Railway Avenue. Both are open 8:00 a.m. to 11:00 p.m. daily.

Tune up   Rebound Cycle (reboundcycle.com) has been a great partner in helping to foster the Alberta bikepacking scene. Find it at the junction of Main Street and 8 Avenue, open Monday to Saturday 10:00 a.m. to 6:00 p.m. and Sunday 10:00 a.m. to 5:00 p.m.

0 km	Begin from the Canmore Civic Centre at 902 7 Avenue. Inside, find the Canmore Museum and Geoscience Centre (cmags.org). $5/person. Open 12:00 to 4:30 p.m. Monday to Friday and 10:00 a.m. to 4:30 p.m. Saturday to Sunday. Turn west on 8 Street, then left on 8 Avenue after one block.
0.7 km	Cross the Bow River bridge and take an immediate left on Three Sisters Path. A Trans Canada Trail kiosk for the "mine side" of the valley is 100 m ahead. First 1.5 km of the path are gravel. Be courteous to pedestrians.
4.2 km	Take left fork, keeping along the Bow River. Sign pointing to Riverside Trail. Short switchback climb in 1 km. Continue straight across Three Sisters Parkway.
6.1 km	Cross Fitzgerald Avenue. A few other intersections are ahead but keep on the path all the way to top of Three Sisters Mountain Village.
7.6 km	At crossing with Stewart Creek Drive, turn left on to the road toward a roundabout. Take the second exit, onto Stewart Creek Rise.
7.7 km	Fork left onto paved path leading behind residential homes and continue along double track trail paralleling the Trans-Canada Highway.
12.1 km	Carefully navigate a creek crossing on a rustic bridge. Cross George Biggy Sr. Road and continue east along The Great Trail (also known as the Trans Canada Trail). Plenty of varied terrain ahead. Expect to be on and off your bike a bunch.

Cross the Trans-Canada Highway for services at Dead Man's Flats. There is a convenience store and a few cafes.

20.0 km	Heart Creek trailhead.
22.8 km	Turn right, up Jewell Pass trail.
24.5 km	Quaite Valley Backcountry Campground. $12/night plus $12 backcountry permit. Book in advance at albertaparks.ca.
24.8 km	Junction. GPS route from a 2016 scout follows a rougher track forking right. A mellower option is now available by bearing left.
25 km	Re-enter Bow Valley Provincial Park at the short climb above the Kananaskis River.
26.4 km	Top out at an elevation of 1613 m. Continue straight.
28.0 km	Cross a bridge over Jewell Creek.
29.3 km	Turn right on Stoney Trail and Barrier Lake comes into view.
29.5 km	Jewell Bay Backcountry Campground. $12/night plus $12 backcountry permit. Must be booked in advance at albertaparks.ca (available mid-June to mid-April). There is a bear box for your food, a communal fire pit with wood, and a pit toilet. For water, hike back down to Barrier Lake. Careful of your footing on the chunky rocks, especially in stiff cycling shoes. Water will need to be treated.

Day 2: Barrier Lake to Lake Minnewanka (140 km)

Today is the Big Kahuna. The allocation of kilometres makes sense when you consider that over half your day is on relatively level asphalt. First, head west along the Front Range gravel rollers, circling north through Cochrane's "western hospitality." You then connect with Highway 40 through a quaint stretch of ranch land alongside the Ghost River. Devil's Gap is your formidable back entrance into the Rocky Mountains. Hike on!

0 km	Turn right, out of Jewell Bay, along Stoney Trail. At an intersection with Jewell Pass trail within 200 m, keep straight.

0.9 km	Fork right along single track beside Barrier Lake. The wider Stoney Trail continues uphill.
2.6 km	Turn right, keeping on the trail across Barrier Lake dam.
4.3 km	Turn left on paved Highway 40.
5.4 km	Turn right on gravel Highway 68 / Sibbald Creek Trail. Gradual 5-km climb ahead.
19 km	Gravel turns to asphalt for the next 23 km.
20.5 km	Sibbald Lake Provincial Campground. $26/night plus $12 reservation fee. Book in advance at albertaparks.ca.
29.8 km	Camp Cadicasu for kids (cadicasu.com) on your left. Sibbald Creek Trail soon curves north.
42.5 km	Go under the Trans-Canada Highway. At a T-junction, turn right, continuing east along Township Road 252. Expect a mix of gravel and asphalt en route to Cochrane. Do not detour from the route unless given express permission. Private property all around.
50.6 km	Gravel turns to asphalt. The Jumping Pound Gas Complex is to the north. JP has been supplying natural gas to Albertans since the early 1950s. Drop down and cross Jumpingpound Creek. Steep climb out.
55.7 km	Turn right on Towers Trail.
61.8 km	Turn right on Rolling Range Road.

| 62.7 km | Turn right on Highway 22, then left across the road and ditch in 100 m. Connect with River Heights Drive. |
| 63.4 km | Turn left down the closed gravel River Heights Rise. Drop down and cross Bow River. |

COCHRANE RECOMMENDATIONS

The route purposely takes advantage of the following services. To bypass Cochrane's humble commercial centre, divert to the Riverview West pedestrian path. Turn left after the bridge and wind along the perimeter of town to Highway 1A.

Java fix   Cochrane Coffee Traders and roastery (coffeetraders.ca) is at 114 2 Avenue West. Plenty of homemade lunch options too.

Restock   Save-On-Foods at 65 Bow Street is the closest grocery store to the route. Open 8:00 a.m. to 10:00 p.m. daily.

Sweet treat   Locally made MacKay's Ice Cream (mackaysicecream.com) is a Cochrane landmark at 220 1 Street West (est. 1948). Open 10:00 a.m. to 6:00 p.m. daily.

Tune up   Bike Bros at 128 River Avenue specializes in mountain bikes and is open at 10:00 a.m. daily. Check www.bikebros.ca for hours.

| 65.9 km | Turn left on 1 Street and head through old downtown. |

66.6 km	Turn right on 4 Avenue, then left on Highway 1A in 200 m. Limited to no shoulder for next 14.6 km. Travel is not recommended in the early or late hours.
81.2 km	Turn right at junction for Highway 40 (also known as Forestry Trunk Road).

GHOST STATION

The Ghost Station convenience store and campground (ghoststation.ca) is 1 km farther along the 1A. Open Monday to Friday 8:00 a.m. to 9:00 p.m.; Saturday and Sunday 9:00 a.m. to 9:00 p.m.

94.9 km	Hamlet of Benchlands. Emergency services building alongside highway.
98.6 km	Hamlet of Waiparous (no services).
103.6 km	Bar C Ranch on your left (closed in 2006).
105.4 km	Highway 40 curves north. Take the next left along unsigned Township Road 270B (TransAlta Road). There is a trailhead sign ahead on the right. Keep on the main gravel road for next 16 km. A few unsigned forest intersections in the area. Popular area for OHV traffic and backcountry camping. Good views from the bench down to the Ghost River valley.
113.4 km	Trappers Hill Campground.
121.8 km	Parking area on the right, followed by a steep gravel descent down to the river. Good opportunity to fill up water bottles and take a bearing. You are looking for the next valley opening to the south — Devil's Gap. Follow faint vehicle tracks along a gravel berm. Be prepared for plenty of hike-a-bike over the next 10 km
123.3 km	There's a sign in the drainage that OHV traffic is not allowed (bikes and hikers are). Enter Banff National Park.
126.4 km	First of three Ghost Lakes en route to Lake Minnewanka. Make your way to the far right (northwest) corner. Likely to be dry.
126.3 km	Second Ghost Lake. Easiest route may be along the water's edge to the left (south). Enter the last narrow channel on the other side.
128.7 km	Third Ghost Lake. Keep an eye out for a more established trail along the north bank of the creek, just before hitting the largest body of water of the three. The trail is a little challenging to find at first. Best bet is to hike/bike along a drainage right to the eastern edge of Lake Minnewanka. You'll more clearly see the trail begin on your right along an elevated outlook. There's a trail sign within 100 m, listing LM20 in 6.8 km. The final stretch will still require hiking through overgrown foliage, plus brief stops to pinpoint where the trail continues. Navigate by inuksuks (stacked rocks) through the chunky drainage beds.
134.5 km	LM22 (Narrows Campground). First of five established backcountry campsites along Lake Minnewanka. A backcountry reservation is required (book in advance at reservation.pc.gc.ca or by phoning 1-877-737-3783). Take any grizzly warnings seriously. Carry bear spray and use the bear bins provided.

Day 3: Lake Minnewanka to Canmore (50 km)

The final single-track stretch around Lake Minnewanka is significantly more rideable than the one on Day 2. Expect a few 70-m pushers, but that's all. The remainder of the route into Canmore is a mix of paved road and smooth Legacy Trail. Built to honour Banff National Park's 125th anniversary, this Canmore connector is one of the world's most utilized pedestrian paths. It sees over 100,000 visitors between early spring and fall. Call it your "cool down."

0 km	Continue west out of LM22.
1.8 km	LM20 (Mount Costigan Campground).
5.5 km	Warden cabin. The trail is much easier to ride beyond this point. It is 15 km to the Lake Minnewanka Day Use Area.
9.3 km	LM11 (Mount Inglismaldie Campground).
10.9 km	LM9 (Aylmer Canyon Campground).
12.3 km	LM8 (Aylmer Pass Junction and Campground).
18.7 km	Cross the Stewart Canyon bridge.
20.1 km	Enter Lake Minnewanka Day Use Area. Black Anchor Snack Shop coming up on your right (likely closed for the season). There used to be a village here, but it is now underwater. There is a large concrete washroom at the junction with Lake Minnewanka Road. Turn left, heading over the dam in 300 m.
24.1 km	Two Jack Lakeside Campground on your left. Book in advance at reservation.pc.gc.ca. Only open until early October.
25.3 km	Keep right at a turn for Johnson Lake.
28.9 km	Turn left on Lake Minnewanka Scenic Drive.
29.5 km	Turn left into Cascade Ponds Day Use Area. Continue south on the connecting trail around ponds. Follow under the Trans-Canada Highway.
30.6 km	Turn left on Rocky Mountain Legacy Trail. Expect to encounter a regular stream of tourists and local riders in the afternoon: 2:00 p.m. is the busiest time.

BANFF

If in need of a quick restock or looking to do some additional sight-seeing, head to the right, approximately 3 km off route. All services.

38.1 km	Washroom and valley viewpoint on your right.
47.6 km	Wapiti Campground on your left. $30/night. First come, first served. Information at wapiticamping.com.
48.4 km	Turn right on Railway Avenue, right on 17 Street, left on 8 Avenue and left on 7 Avenue.
49.7 km	Finish at the Civic Centre.

CANMORE RECOMMENDATIONS

Brew   Finish your ride with a local brew at the Canmore Brewing Company (canmorebrewing.com), established in 2016, just ahead on your right at 1460 Railway Avenue. Open 2:00 to 7:00 p.m. Wednesday and Thursday; 1:00 to 8:00 p.m. Friday and Saturday; and 1:00 to 6:00 p.m. on Sunday.

Foood!   Rocky Mountain Bagel Co. (thebagel.ca/menu.php) is a favourite lunch stop. Its 102 830 Main Street location is open 6:00 a.m. to 6:00 p.m. daily.

Go an extra day?   The Montane Traverse (on the "sunny side" of the valley) and Highline Trail (the "mine side" of the valley) are two popular loops around town. Trail maps can be downloaded from Bike Canmore at bikecanmore.ca.

* Additional Canmore recommendations can be found in Trip 2, High Rockies.

5. HIGHWOOD

START AND FINISH   Coleman, Alberta

WHO SHOULD RIDE?   A challenging route that favours a strong climber, patience in potentially mucky conditions (sharing tracks with ohv vehicles), backcountry savvy and seasoned hike-a-bike muscles. Day 1 is the hardest.

DISTANCE   357 km

ELEVATION GAIN   5522 m

SUGGESTED NUMBER OF DAYS   3

About the Route

Highwood is a looped route through the Elk and Livingstone mountain valleys in southern Alberta. Riders will be immersed in coal-mining history, get to test their mettle on the first substantial climb of the Great Divide Mountain Bike Route, camp at the headwaters of the Elbow River, then grind out the last few gravel miles of Highway 40 — originating 1027 km north in Grande Prairie.

   The crown jewel of the route is Highwood Pass, the highest paved climb in all of Canada.

Getting to Coleman   The nearest international airport is in Calgary. From there, head 242 km south along Highway 22 through the windy foothills to Crowsnest Pass. If you are driving in, inquire about parking on one of the quiet residential streets. Town bylaws may allow you to park for up to 72 hours unless signs tell you otherwise. The Shell gas station also has a large gravel parking area. Ask about overnight parking.

ELEVATION PROFILE

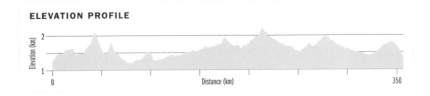

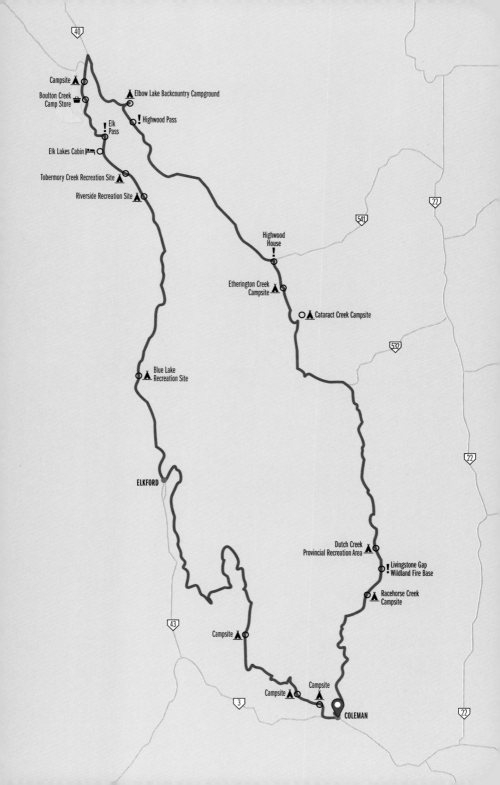

40

Campsite

Boulton Creek
Camp Store

Elbow Lake Backcountry Campground

Highwood Pass

Elk
Pass

Elk Lakes Cabin

Tobermory Creek Recreation Site

Riverside Recreation Site

541

Highwood
House

Etherington Creek
Campsite

Cataract Creek Campsite

532

Blue Lake
Recreation Site

22

ELKFORD

Dutch Creek
Provincial Recreation Area

Livingstone Gap
Wildland Fire Base

22

Racehorse Creek
Campsite

43

Campsite

Campsite

Campsite

3

COLEMAN

22

Important note from Teck Coal Mines "Our mine boundaries change each year and have the potential to influence access to any of your routes in the Elk Valley. Please refer to the Teck website and/or the ministry access management maps before setting out on any future ride." You can review Teck's boundary maps at teck.com/elkvalleymaps.

When to go Head out after June 15 to take advantage of the Elbow Lake backcountry campground.

Day 1: Coleman to Elkford (104 km)

My initial scout spat me out onto Teck Coal Mining private property (at 52 km). What could have been a confrontational encounter with a security guard turned into an enlightening share. "We often have Divide riders getting lost on our property," she told me (of the Line Creek Road junction). This statement was quickly followed by, "But you came from somewhere else?" I later followed up with a GPX file and got approval for this route.

An early start is recommended to allow plenty of time for a challenging day ahead. There will be several slow sections with plenty of hike-a-bike.

COLEMAN RECOMMENDATIONS

Java fix   The Cinnamon Bear Cafe is open at 7:30 a.m. Monday to Saturday; 10:00 a.m. on Sunday. At this writing, the cafe serves locally roasted Crowsnest Coffee (by fellow mountain biker Troy Misseghers). Grab a cup of the popular Bushtown blend and a homemade cinnamon bun to go. Be prepared for lineups at peak times! A popular stop for tourists driving through.

Local intel   The United Riders of Crowsnest (uroc.ca) are a good resource for local trails and events.

Sleep on the cheap   The nearest campsite is Lost Lemon Campground (lostlemon.com) in Blairmore for $30/night. Any of the motel options in the area are going to run you $100 on a good day, closer to $200 if you book last minute. You can find better value at a local B&B. Country Encounters in Coleman is a personal favourite: $109 for their least expensive room, which includes cookies and coffee through the evening, plus a tremendous home-cooked breakfast in the morning.

Stock up There are a few convenience stores located along the highway. For a more substantial grocery run, hit up the IGA in Blairmore.

Tune up Alpenland (alpenland.ca), est. 2016, is the only bicycle shop in the Crowsnest Pass region. It is located down the highway in the commercial hub of Blairmore. Open 10:00 a.m. to 6:00 p.m. Tuesday through Saturday. Call ahead to make sure they can help you. Any specialty parts may require a trip to Fernie.

0 km	Begin south from the intersection of 86 Street and Crowsnest Highway. Keep right on 16 Avenue (which becomes 80 Street). This route avoids riding on the busy highway. Follow your GPS, as cues can get confusing.
0.9 km	Turn right on 79 Street (which becomes 18 Avenue, then 71 Street).
2 km	Turn left on 18 Avenue.
2.8 km	Cross Crowsnest Highway and continue uphill on 66 Street. Keep left on 22 Avenue, then right up 63 Street.

6 km	Hydro corridor running perpendicular to your path. Left takes you straight up the hill. The second left, 200 m ahead, rounds through a Crown camping area on an easier switchback up. Head this way.
6.8 km	Top out and begin west on an inactive road. This rough OHV track parallels the hydro corridor for next 4 km. Expect a mud bog if it's been raining; also some steep bike pushing.
10.2 km	Right at an unsigned T-junction for Allison Creek Road. There's a power substation at the corner.
13.4 km	Turn left down an unsigned OHV trail. The path curves left across a small creek in 1 km. A bridge may be present.
19.7 km	Keep right at a junction for Deadman Pass Trail. In 100 m, cross into British Columbia. Trail signs present as you descend a rough trail with runoff water.
22 km	Cross over a creek with a bridge out (watch your footing). In 200 m, rejoin a logging road. Turn left, heading downhill, and follow this all the way to the valley floor.
24.8 km	Turn right on unsigned Alexander Creek Road, heading north on a slight uphill. To the west is Mt. Erikson.
31.8 km	Keep on the right fork and cross a bridge over Alexander Creek.

32.8 km	Turn left off the main road and begin a long, gradual climb up Soap Creek Trail. Several hike-a-bikes likely over the next 9 km.
36 km	Turn left. Straight continues to an open field that dead ends ahead.
38.6 km	Take the left fork.
41.3 km	Fork right. Private 4WD track, heading left.
42.5 km	Switchback up to a clearing in the trees. Here starts the most difficult climb on the route. Top out at 2175 m.
46 km	The road curves wide left, continuing downhill.
52.3 km	Continue straight, then go left at a junction with an unsigned forestry road. Do not stray from the outlined route (this is still Teck territory). The road curves back south around Mt. Erris.
62.6 km	At a junction with an unsigned forestry road, go right and follow the valley floor out.
69 km	Right again at a junction with an unsigned forestry road.
73.4 km	Left at a fork, heading downhill. Right continues to Grove Lake.
75.3 km	Cross over train tracks and turn right at a junction for Valley Forest Service Road.
80 km	Keep *straight* across paved Line Creek Road (where those Divide riders are getting lost), continuing on Sulphur Spring Forest Service Road. You are now on the Great Divide Mountain Bike Route. Several forestry road offshoots over the next 20 km. Keep an eye on your GPS.
81.1 km	Cross a bridge over the Fording River.
83.4 km	Take left fork.
90.7 km	Take right fork, heading uphill. Good views of the Elk Valley.
95.6 km	On your left will be a signed intersection for Lost Lake. Some 120 m farther, turn right down a possibly overgrown single track through a meadow. Again, keep watching your GPS.
96.7 km	Go left on an intersecting forest service road. Continuing straight on single track takes you down to Josephine Falls overlook, 100 m off route. It is worth the detour!
98.1 km	A road comes in from over your left shoulder. Keep straight.
99.2 km	Keep right at a fork. In 500 m, turn left on Fording River Road. Enjoy a nice, paved descent into Elkford.

| 103.6 km | Turn right at an intersection for Elk Valley Highway. There's a RaceTrac Gas and car wash on the corner. |
| 104 km | Elkford Municipal Campground is on the right. $20/night with free showers. Walking distance to most services. |

ELKFORD RECOMMENDATIONS (EVENING)

A small coal-mining town with basic services, all within a kilometre. Full directory at elkford.ca.

Indoor accommodation   Weather-weary Divide riders have been known to fill the Elkford Motor Inn (elkfordmotorinn.com) on Day 1. Pub, cafe and laundry on site.

Foood!   For the rider with an iron gut, order up a Coal Miner pizza at Kapps. The pie has three types of meat, onions, olives and banana peppers. Located at 418 Boivin Road, Kapps is open 7:30 a.m. to 10:00 p.m. most days. They close an hour earlier on Sunday.

Restock   Elkford mini-mart and RaceTrac Gas are easy go-tos for Divide riders blazing through. They are located across from each other at the Fording River junction. The gas station also has a car wash. A more substantial restock can be found at the Kootenay Market, located across from the campground, open 10:00 a.m. to 8:00 p.m. daily.

Day 2: Elkford to Elbow Lake (103 km)

Our vehicle support crew on the Great Divide Mountain Bike Tour would have to take a 367-km front-country detour around this Elk Pass "shortcut" (into Peter Lougheed Provincial Park). Memories from the route include an annual mocking of my "net downhill" description (the reverse for you), huddling around a fire in the Tobermory Creek cabin after encountering unexpected snow in August, and being spooked by a large moose while racing the Tour Divide in 2015. Your second big climb up to Highwood Pass will seem relatively straightforward in comparison. Take it easy on the road cyclists!

ELKFORD RECOMMENDATIONS (MORNING)

Java fix Emi's (located in the Elkford Motor Inn) has the "best breakfast in town," including steak and eggs. Open at 7:00 a.m.

0 km	Leaving the Elkford municipal campground, head to the right, along the Elk Valley Highway (43). The road turns to gravel as you leave town. Continue straight unless otherwise directed. Follow the Great Divide Mountain Bike Route for the next 87 km. Begin a "net uphill" to Elk Pass.
45.2 km	Cross a bridge over the Elk River and begin up the east side of the valley.
46 km	Fork left, continuing north at an intersection. The track will begin weaving in and out of a hydro corridor.
56.2 km	Riverside camping area on the left.
62.6 km	Rustic Tobermory Creek Forest Service Cabin is on your right. First come first served, with metal cots and a wood-burning stove.
67.6 km	Fork right and begin a more substantial climb. Left continues to the Alpine Club of Canada's Elk Lakes Cabin (alpineclubof-canada.ca/web/ACCMember/Huts/Elk_Lakes_Cabin.aspx). Walk-in campsites are available for $5/night. Access is 550 m from this intersection. Part of Elk Lakes Provincial Park.
71.6 km	Top out at Elk Pass (1905 m) and enter Alberta. Elkford once proposed extending Highway 43 up and over the pass, but the idea was nixed because of environmental concerns. The trail soon turns left into the trees and begins a steeper descent.

PHOTO: JEFF BARTLETT

	At the bottom, fork to the right, heading back up to the hydro corridor. Left is an alternative loop up Elk Pass.
77.8 km	Enter the trailhead parking lot for Elk Pass. Continue to the right, on Kananaskis Lakes Trail. The route is paved for the next 66 km.
80 km	Whiskey Jack pedestrian crossing is marked in white across the road. Turn right for services and camping at Boulton Creek. The main route continues straight.

BOULTON CREEK SERVICES

Stock up for the remainder of the journey, just in case Highwood House (65 km ahead) is closed. Camping and $2 showers are available; open early May to mid-October. Exact hours of the camp store are difficult to pin down.

83.7 km	At the top of a nasty rise is Elkwood Campground.
86.3 km	Peter Lougheed Provincial Park information centre is on your right. Lougheed served as premier of Alberta from 1971 to 1985.
87.5 km	Continue past a junction with Highway 742 and head up to Highway 40 (Kananaskis Trail).
89.8 km	Turn right on Highway 40. Pass through snow gates and begin a 17-km ascent to Highwood Pass.
102 km	Stop just short of the pass and turn left up Elbow Lake Trail. Mountain biking allowed.
103.4 km	Arrive at the Elbow Lake Backcountry Campground. Open June 15 to November 30. Sites are $12/night plus $12 backcountry permit; reserve well in advance at albertaparks.ca. Elbow Lake is the headwaters for the Elbow River, one of the sources of Calgary's drinking water. If you have energy to burn, take on the 3-km trek up to (receding) Rae Glacier.

Day 3: Elbow Lake to Coleman (150 km)

From the top of Highwood Pass, begin a lengthy paved descent to Highwood House. Your final stretch of gravel flows alongside the Livingstone Range, the

eastern wall of the Rockies, named after Scottish explorer David Livingstone. There are plenty of creek crossings, backcountry campsites and quaint grazing lands to hold your attention on the afternoon climbs. Best experienced at the golden hour.

0 km	Head back down to the Elbow Lake trailhead and turn left on Highway 40.
6.3 km	Top out at Highwood Pass (2206 m). Begin a rolling 38-km descent.
44.3 km	Turn right on gravel Highway 940 (closed December–May) and cross a bridge over the Highwood River. Keep straight unless otherwise directed. There are several gravel offshoots from here until Coleman.

HIGHWOOD HOUSE

Highwood House at the junction. The service station typically has some grocery items.

50.2 km	Continue straight on the main route, uphill. Left heads to Etherington Creek Campground.
57.5 km	Cross Cataract Creek. Campsites are across from day-use area, approximately 900 m off route. Do not depend on water pumps. Always a good idea to carry your own filtration system. There are plenty of creeks and rivers to draw from in the valley.
59.2 km	Cross Wilkinson Creek. Cross it again in 2 km.

67 km	Begin a 4-km climb, the first of two big pushes on today's route.
71 km	Net downhill for the next 49 km.
76.6 km	At a signed junction with Highway 532, keep right. Left goes to the town of Nanton (74 km off route).
80.8 km	Cross through red metal gates (road closed from December 10 to April 30).
86.5 km	Signed turnoff for Livingstone Falls Provincial Recreation Area. Continue straight across Livingstone River in 900 m.
88.8 km	On your left is Blue Bronna Wilderness Camp (bluebronna.org), operated by a Christian non-profit.
105.1 km	Keep straight at a junction for Oldman River Campground and descend to river crossing.
110.9 km	Dutch Creek Campground is on your left.
113.8 km	Livingstone Gap Wildland Fire Base. Possible help in case of emergency. Pay phone on site.
116.2 km	Keep straight at a junction with Maycroft Road. Left follows the Oldman River east through the Livingstone Gap, eventually connecting with Highway 22.
120.1 km	Racehorse Provincial Recreation Area on your right. Begin a rolling 19-km climb, the last big push.
138 km	Top out and begin a net downhill to Coleman.
140.9 km	Keep straight at a restricted road.
147.3 km	Enter the outskirts of Coleman. Stay on Highway 40 to its terminus.
150.4 km	Finish at the intersection with Crowsnest Highway (3).

COLEMAN RECOMMENDATIONS

Foood! Grab a pint and homemade burger from The Rum Runner (therumrunner.ca), located 750 m west. The restaurant and bar are named for the Alberta prohibition era (1916–1923). During that time, booze was illegally transported through Crowsnest Pass from Fernie to Pincher Creek. Hours are 11:30 a.m. to 10:00 p.m., Monday through Thursday; 11:30 a.m. to 11:00 p.m., Friday to Sunday.

6. CASTLE

START AND FINISH **Blairmore, Alberta**

WHO SHOULD RIDE? **All riders can complete the first and last day without issue. Day 2 is the most challenging as far as backcountry terrain, unsigned routes, hike-a-bike and a challenging descent into the West Castle valley.**

DISTANCE **266 km**

ELEVATION GAIN **4566 m**

SUGGESTED NUMBER OF DAYS **3**

About the Route

Castle is the most interesting route from a conservation standpoint.

Head down the foothills from Crowsnest Pass to Waterton Lakes National Park (a UNESCO World Heritage Site). This southwestern Alberta region has a certain golden charm, encompassing rolling foothills, quaint farmland and panoramic prairie views.

Skirting along the U.S. border westward through Akamina–Kishinena Provincial Park, you soon find yourself along a quiet backcountry track, relatively devoid of the forestry and mining operations you might expect in such a resource rich region. This lack of industry is because of the neighbouring Flathead Valley and the newly formed (as of February 16, 2017) Castle Provincial Park. Both are key pieces in a wildlife corridor that extends from Wyoming to northern Canada. Learn more about the Yellowstone to Yukon initiative at y2y.net, and of the fight to keep the Flathead wild at wildsight.ca.

ELEVATION PROFILE

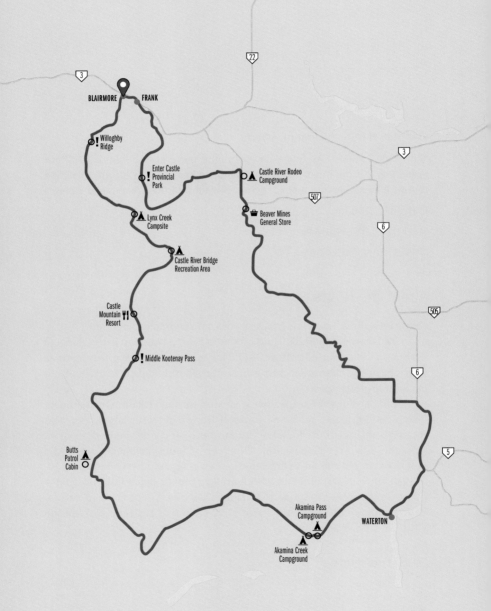

BLAIRMORE FRANK

Willoghby
Ridge

Enter Castle
Provincial
Park

Castle River Rodeo
Campground

Beaver Mines
General Store

Lynx Creek
Campsite

Castle River Bridge
Recreation Area

Castle
Mountain
Resort

Middle Kootenay Pass

Butts
Patrol
Cabin

Akamina Pass
Campground

WATERTON

Akamina Creek
Campground

3

22

3

507

6

505

6

5

Note: Following massive wildfires in recent years, there was significant damage to the Akamina Pass Trail and Akamina–Kishinena Provincial Park (Day 2). Trail work was underway in 2019. Be sure to inquire about conditions before setting out. The route can be ridden as a point-to-point should any sections need to be omitted.

Best time to go   September 1–15. Miss the busy tourist season in Waterton Lakes National Park and take advantage of the early autumn colours. Final day for many businesses (and restock potential) in the park is the last weekend of September.

Getting to Blairmore   The nearest international airport is Calgary. Head 236 km south along Highway 22 through windy foothills to Crowsnest Pass.

Day 1: Blairmore to Waterton (122 km)

This stretch is one of my favourite finds. You have a 9-km gradual climb out of Frank within the first hour. The route then meanders along the foothills to Waterton. Leave a little early to avoid the strong regional winds. Once they begin to kick, oh boy!

BLAIRMORE RECOMMENDATIONS

Blairmore is the commercial hub for the Crowsnest Pass region. Most services are located just down from the Crowsnest Highway (3), along 20 Avenue.

Bike shop   Alpenland Ski and Sports (alpenland.ca) is the only bike shop in the Crowsnest and is located at 13131 20 Avenue. Open 10:00 a.m. to 6:00 p.m., Tuesday through Saturday.

Got an extra day?   Connect with the United Riders of Crowsnest (uroc.ca). This club is a great resource for local riding knowledge and events.

Java fix   Stone's Throw Café (stonesthrowcafe.ca) is rated the #1 restaurant in Blairmore on TripAdvisor. Great eats, locally roasted coffee and an ambassador of local trail culture. Open Monday to Friday 8:00 a.m. to 4:00 p.m.; Saturday from 8:00 a.m. to 5:00 p.m.; and Sunday from 10:00 a.m. to 4:00 p.m. Located at 13019 20 Avenue.

Sleep on the cheap   Check out Lost Lemon Campground (lostlemon.com). $30/night. WiFi, showers, firewood and a small convenience store on site.

Stock up   The IGA grocery store is across the street from Lost Lemon Campground at the west end of town. Open 9:00 a.m. to 9:00 p.m. daily.

---

0 km   From the corner of 133 Street, head east on 20 Avenue (the main street). In 400 m, connect with the pedestrian path heading under Highway 3. Soon enter the neighbouring town of Frank. Limited services.

1.6 km   Turn left onto Crowsnest Highway 3.

2.4 km   Turn right on 150 Street, then a quick left on 152 Street (Crowsnest Heritage Route). The road turns to gravel in view of Turtle Mountain and the Frank rockslide. On April 29, 1903, at 4:10 a.m., the mining town was buried by 110 million tonnes of rock. Visit the interpretive centre back in town on 153 Street.

5.9 km   Turn left at a T-junction with 9 Avenue. Continue up through a residential area.

7.3 km   Fork left on 232 Street.

PHOTO: MATTHEW CLARK

9.2 km	Turn right on gravel Adanac Road, heading uphill.
18 km	Top out with a great view of the Carbondale River valley. Descend into Castle Provincial Park.
23.2 km	Take the left fork, heading east along Township Road 61A. Follow Carbondale / Castle River valley out of the mountains.
25.4 km	Keep right. Sightlines are limited along this narrower stretch. Watch for trucks and campers headed in your direction.
30.4 km	Keep straight.
39.6 km	Turn right on paved Highway 507.
41.4 km	Castle River Rodeo Campground is on your left.
44.8 km	Continue straight through a junction where Highway 507 heads east for Pincher Creek.
46 km	Village of Beaver Mines.

BEAVER MINES GENERAL STORE

Beaver Mines General Store (beaverminesstore.ca) is open 7:00 a.m. to 7:00 p.m., daily. Locals meet for coffee when the store opens. The store provides a good opportunity to learn a little bit about this coal-mining hamlet, now seeing a resurgence due to interest in Castle Mountain Resort. The village's population once hovered around 1,500 but now sits at 80.

46.4 km	Turn left on Range Road 22A. Watch your GPS here, as there are several turns and road-name changes coming up.
48.7 km	Keep left on Township Road 60, heading uphill. The road curves past Grumpy's Greenhouses.
51.1 km	Keep left on Township Road 55A.
52.2 km	Turn right on Range Road 21A.
54.9 km	Take the left fork along Range Road 22A, heading downhill across the river. Stay straight through a Shell work area.
58.4 km	The road curves left, heading downhill across Mill Creek.
61.2 km	At the Shell plant on the right, keep straight. The road drops down again to the creek.
62.4 km	Take the left fork, climbing 4 km hard uphill.
66 km	Top out. Nice overlook at a cable fence guard.
72 km	T-intersection and a group of buildings at the bottom of a hill. Turn left and stay on the main road as it dips across a creek and heads uphill.
73.5 km	Nearing the top of a hill, turn right at a small reservoir.
74.9 km	Go left across a small bridge, then uphill.
79.9 km	Turn left, then make a quick right in 700 m (heading uphill).
84 km	Fork right, then right again in 800 m.
87.4 km	Fork right on Range Road 303.
89.2 km	Turn left on Township Road 34.

94.1 km	Turn right on Range Road 300.
97.4 km	Left on Range Road 32.
100.6 km	Turn right on paved Highway 6. Watch for early evening traffic and higher winds as you navigate the narrow shoulder.
112.4 km	Turn right on Highway 5 and pass through Waterton Lakes National Park gate. Paved Kootenai Brown Trail soon begins on the opposite side of the road.
120.6 km	Path meets up with the site of the old Waterton Visitor Centre. Continue down the highway. The new Visitor Centre is currently under construction within the Waterton townsite, scheduled to open in spring 2021. A good resource if you plan to spend an extra day in the area.
121.2 km	Turn left on Mountain View Road and head into the quaint town centre. Continue all the way to the end of the street, then turn right on Windflower Avenue.

WATERTON RECOMMENDATIONS (EVENING)

Most services close in the national park by the last week of September. Visit mywaterton.ca for current info.

Foood! Wieners of Waterton (wienersofwaterton.com) is the #1 local restaurant on TripAdvisor. The Taco Bar (watertontacos. wixsite.com/thetacobar) is also great for casual dining. Both locations generally close around 9:00 p.m.

Gear up Tamarack Outdoor Outfitters (hikewaterton.com) carries a good selection of outdoor gear. Headlights, base layers, sandals for walking around camp — that sort of thing. A good opportunity to also ask about local hikes. There are no dedicated bike shops in town. The novelty bikes (tandems and surreys) that you see tourists riding are from the store called Pat's Waterton (patswaterton.com), which only has rentals.

Restock Rocky Mountain Foodmart is your go-to for groceries. Open 8:00 a.m. to 10:00 p.m. If the selection has been picked over, you may need to pull together a combination of food items from the touristy shops and restaurants around town. Pack enough to get you to Blairmore.

122.2 km The Townsite Campground can be booked online using Parks Canada's reservation service at reservation.pc.gc.ca. Make sure not to leave any food lying around. The area is known for aggressive deer. Also, do not forget your tent pegs! All sites are exposed to Waterton's infamous winds.

Day 2: Waterton to Castle Mountain (97 km)

Exiting Waterton, make your presence known as you descend Akamina Pass. The Flathead region has one of the highest concentrations of grizzly bears in North America. That said, I have only ever seen one small black bear here — consider this an optimistic disclaimer. The ride back across the Alberta boundary will make for an epic happy-hour photo.

WATERTON RECOMMENDATIONS (MORNING)

Java fix For the early riser, Starbucks Glacier Bistro inside the Bayshore Inn (www.bayshoreinn.com) tends to be the first open, at 7:00 a.m. My suggestion would be to head over to Pearls café (pearlscafe.ca), which serves up Cuppers Coffee, roasted in Lethbridge (cuppers.ca). They also have fresh, home-baked goods, and specialize in lunches to go. Both have free WiFi for customers.

0 km	Double back 1300 m to Akamina Parkway (Range Road 302A). Turn left, heading uphill. The first 15.5 km of the route is paved.
9.1 km	Historic site of the first oil well in western Canada (1902) is on your left.
15.5 km	Turn right, up Akamina Pass Trail. You are about to enter remote territory. Do you have bear spray? Enough food? This is the only legal off-road cycling route in or out of Waterton Lakes National Park.
16.6 km	Akamina Pass Backcountry Campground at Akamina Pass. Enter Akamina–Kishinena Provincial Park and the province of British Columbia.
17.9 km	Akamina Creek Backcountry Campground. The path down from here is not well maintained and may be chewed up from waterflow and horse tracks. The route was built in the 1920s and parallels Akamina Creek.
29.1 km	The path widens and becomes Kishinena Creek Road.
29.9 km	At a three-way junction, head left over a bridge. The trail widens further.
38.5 km	Bridge back over Kishinena Creek.
46.5 km	Keep straight at a path heading down to the creek.
49.6 km	The road curves around the base of Miskwasini Peak. Looking south from the top, you are approximately 100 m from the U.S. (unpatrolled) border and Glacier National Park. There are several forestry offshoots in the Flathead Valley ahead. Keep straight unless otherwise directed.
61.2 km	Forestry operations on your left. Drop down and cross a bridge over Sage Creek.
67.8 km	Turn right at a trail sign for Commerce Creek Road. If you're in a bind and need to stay the night, Butts Patrol Cabin is approximately 1 km off route. Check your GPS.
72.4 km	Turn left down an unsigned road. Commerce Creek continues straight.
79.9 km	Cross the creek (bridge out). Continue right, heading uphill. There are trapping signs alongside the trail.
81.4 km	Take a right fork onto an OHV trail over a hump. The trail soon curves left through a narrow valley. As you gradually ascend, look for an exposed red ridge to the northeast. You are heading there! Be particularly bear-aware in this area and make lots of noise.

86.6 km	At an opening, take the right-hand fork, continuing uphill.
88.2 km	Exit the treeline along a rolling uphill track to Middle Kootenay Pass (Alberta boundary).
89.3 km	Top out at 1938 m. Tremendous view of the West Castle valley ahead. Path down can be a little confusing at first. At a fork in 400 m, keep left.
90.6 km	Cross over a good stream for water, then go through a metal gate in 100 m. Follow orange snowmobile signs down a rougher trail. You may want to hike with your bike.
91.7 km	Keep left at an opening in the trees.
94.6 km	Keep left on less primitive Range Road 40A, following the valley floor north.
97.3 km	Castle Mountain Resort is on your left.

CASTLE MOUNTAIN RECOMMENDATIONS

Food and accommodation availability are difficult to pin down in the summer (likelihood increases on weekends and after July 1). The resort is currently working on a new development master plan that includes mountain biking. Do not plan on this being a restock, just a welcome diversion if anything is open — the T-Bar Pub for hot pizza and cold beer, perhaps. Indoor accommodations can be booked in advance. Check current details at skicastle.ca.

Sleep on the cheap Wild camping is permitted anywhere outside the resort and the Castle Wetlands (~1 km on either side of the resort). This situation will likely evolve as the provincial park confirms its recreation plan. The next established campground is at Castle River Bridge, 12 km ahead. Book online at albertaparks.ca. Unserviced sites are $32/night plus $12 reservation fee.

Day 3: Castle Mountain to Blairmore (47 km)

My original scout was quite a bit more convoluted than what you see here. At 20 km, my instincts took me left (you turn right) in search of a path less travelled, which soon became a complicated network of OHV trails looping northwest, ultimately back around to Lyons Creek Road. My suggestion is to stick to the main route and enjoy a relatively straightforward last hurrah into

PHOTO: MATTHEW CLARK

Blairmore. Two short but challenging climbs to contend with today, both of them along wide gravel roads.

0 km	Continue north from Castle Mountain Resort along paved Highway 774.
8.9 km	Take the bridge over the West Castle River. Syncline Group Camping Area is ahead on your left.
11.3 km	Turn left after sign for Lynx Creek Campground (9 km from here) on Castle Falls Road.
12.1 km	Cross the West Castle River. Campground is on your right.
13.2 km	Go left at O'Hagen Road, heading uphill. Sweat it out for the next 2 km.
20.9 km	Turn right at a T-intersection (with trail kiosk) and head east along Carbondale River Road. Lynx Creek Campground 1300 m ahead.
22.5 km	Turn left on Lynx Creek Road. Continue a gradual ascent to the valley floor.
32.3 km	At an unsigned junction for Goat Creek Road, Lynx Creek Road becomes Lyons Creek Road and begins a steady 5-km climb up to Willoughby Ridge. Here you cross the Great Divide hiking trail, stretching 1120 km north from the U.S. border at Waterton Lakes National Park to Kakwa Provincial Park near Prince George, BC.
37.4 km	Top out and begin a 9-km gradual descent to the outskirts of Blairmore.
46.7 km	Turn left at the T-junction for 132 Street. In three blocks, turn right at the T-junction for 19 Avenue. Ahead one more block, turn left on 133 Street, heading over the train tracks.
47.2 km	Finish at the intersection with 20 Avenue (main street).

BEN WONG'S

Foood! Check out the lunch buffet at Ben Wong's located at 13249 20 Avenue. Open 11:00 a.m. to 2:00 p.m. Tuesday through Friday.

7. TOP OF THE WORLD

START AND FINISH   Cranbrook, British Columbia

WHO SHOULD RIDE?   Plenty of rugged and remote climbs that are generally reserved for OHV horsepower. The elevation gain is second only to the Front Range. Pack light!

DISTANCE   347 km

ELEVATION GAIN   5891 m

SUGGESTED NUMBER OF DAYS   4

About the Route

If I had to pick one route to showcase both the grandeur and the extreme physicality of bikepacking in the Canadian Rockies, Top of the World would be it.

Much of the inspiration for this route comes from the annual Kootenay Gravel Grinder, now called The Lost Elephant (lostelephant.ca). James McKee of Favorit Cycles in Cranbrook organized the inaugural event in 2015 in honour of fallen Kimberley rider Brad Fuller. The Great Divide finisher was killed by an avalanche while backcountry skiing in the Meachen Creek area on February 28, 2015. Brad and I had shared a few adventurous conversations over the years. It is a terrible shame, what happened. I would also like to give a special acknowledgment to Brad's father, Bob, who was an integral part of my Race Across America crew in 2008. He passed on Christmas Day 2016.

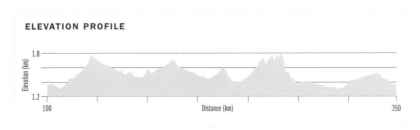

ELEVATION PROFILE

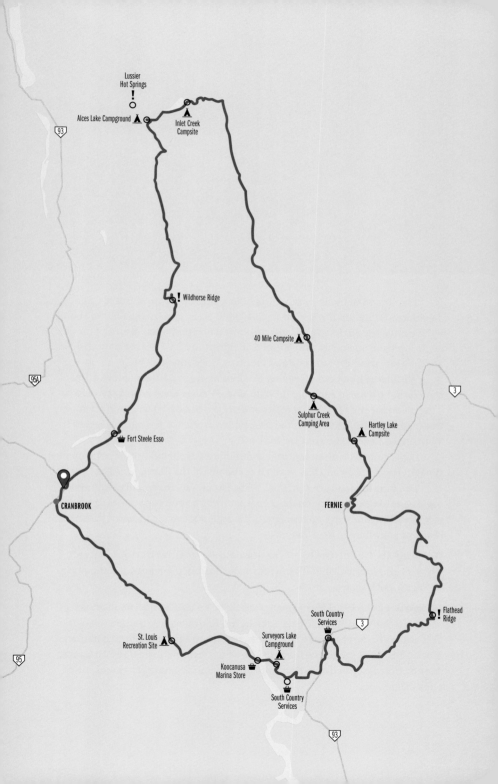

Lussier
Hot Springs

Alces Lake Campground

Inlet Creek
Campsite

93

Wildhorse Ridge

40 Mile Campsite

95A

Sulphur Creek
Camping Area

Hartley Lake
Campsite

3

Fort Steele Esso

CRANBROOK

FERNIE

95

St. Louis
Recreation Site

South Country
Services

Surveyors Lake
Campground

Flathead
Ridge

3

Koocanusa
Marina Store

South Country
Services

93

The Gravel Grinder was the first bikepacking event in western Canada. James keeps it pretty low key on social media, in case you haven't heard about it. "We understand that people want to start when they want to start. You can begin anytime on Friday, July 22, or Saturday, July 23. For that matter, do it anytime and post up your time and pictures," he wrote in 2016.

Within the first hour of leaving Cranbrook, begin a 32-km climb to Top of the World Provincial Park via the Wild Horse Valley. Keep a close eye on your GPS as you ascend old logging roads and overgrown OHV trails, and question uncertain directions through the precarious drainage. A lengthy descent to Whiteswan Lake is your reward for Day 1.

Days 2 and 3 bring an increasing number of challenging climbs through the Bull River valley and the western perimeter of the Flathead Valley.

The final lowland stretch is across the Kootenay River and up the gravel backroads to Cranbrook. Finishing on a patio in the afternoon sun is a mandatory cue. Environment Canada reports the region as having the most sunshine hours of anywhere in BC. Cheers!

Getting to Cranbrook   Canadian Rockies International Airport (flyyxc.com) has inbound flights four to seven days/week from Vancouver, Kelowna and Calgary.

Where does the Wild Horse get its name?   In 1863 a small flood of miners occupied the Wild Horse Creek area in the Kootenays, so named when the first miners to the area saw a wild horse near the mouth and followed it up the creek. This was a rough and ready camp, which an unpublished 1967 doctoral dissertation described as "a horde of outlaw gamblers, murderers and out-of-a-job desperados."

Day 1: Cranbrook to Whiteswan Lake (87 km)

Half your day will be a slog up the Wild Horse River valley to an alpine region adjacent to Top of the World Provincial Park. The other half will be enjoying a descent to Whiteswan Lake. Somewhere in the middle, as you push your bike along on a narrowing OHV track, you may wonder, "Is this the right trail?" You are now part of a long line of people — explorers, miners, loggers and indigenous Ktunaxa — who likely uttered a similar sentiment at some point. Getting a little lost helps bring us back to a primal state of being. And that's OK! Just keep watching your GPS.

CRANBROOK RECOMMENDATIONS

Cranbrook is the urban centre for the East Kootenay region. All services are here. More information at cranbrook.ca.

Java fix   The Kootenay Roasting Company (krccoffee.com) is at 903 Baker Street, the heart of Cranbrook's quiet downtown. Open 8:00 a.m. to 5:30 p.m. Monday through Thursday and 9:00 a.m. to 5:00 p.m. on Saturday. Closed Sunday.

Sleep on the cheap   Mount Baker RV Park is located away from the highway at 1501 1 Street South. Tent sites are $26/night. They have WiFi, laundry and hot showers. Book in advance at mountbakerrvpark.com.

Stock up   There are several grocery stores in town. The Real Canadian Superstore at 2100 17 Street North is closest to the start. Open 8:00 a.m. to 10:00 p.m. daily. Make sure to carry enough calories to get you to Fernie.

Tune up   Gerick Sports, at 320 Cranbrook Street North, is open 9:30 a.m. to 6:00 p.m. Monday to Friday and 9:30 a.m. to 5:30 p.m. on Saturday (gericksports.com).

0 km	Begin at the Cranbrook Visitor Centre at 2279 Cranbrook Street North (cranbrooktourism.com). Check online for hours. Turn left on Highway 3/95 and carefully navigate west (no shoulder). Turn right on 30 Avenue in 350 m, then immediately left on the Stahl frontage road. Keep left at next two gravel forks.
1.1 km	Trailhead for the Isadore Canyon Trail / Trans Canada Trail. Continue straight for 600 m. At the hydro corridor, turn left on

a two-track across the ditch. Turn right on Highway 95. A better shoulder now exists.

6.3 km	Take the exit for Highway 93/95 North toward Invermere and Radium.
13.3 km	Cross over the Kootenay River. Look for the 1890s Fort Steele Heritage town (fortsteele.ca) on the bluff to your left. The route climbs from here all the way to Wild Horse Pass, 32 km ahead.
14.5 km	Turn right on Wardner / Fort Steele Road.

FORT STEELE RESORT & RV PARK

The Fort Steele Resort & RV Park (fortsteele.com) and Esso is at the highway junction. Open 7:00 a.m. to 8:00 p.m. daily and 8:00 a.m. to 8:00 p.m. Sunday. Your next opportunity to purchase food is in Fernie.

14.8 km	Turn left on Wildhorse Forest Service Road. The track turns to gravel and begins a more substantial kick up the Wild Horse River valley. Expect to encounter OHV enthusiasts.
16.9 km	Stay straight on the main road. There's an unsigned branch to the left.
19.7 km	Keep right around a bend. Unsigned road continues straight. In 600 m, keep straight at an unsigned turn for Lakit Lookout Road.
20 km	On your right is the Wild Horse Creek Historic Site and interpretive trail. Check out ruins of the previously mentioned 1864 gold-rush town.
21.7 km	Keep right at a fork, to continue along the lower path through the river valley. The track begins to narrow, with more unsigned turns. Keep straight unless otherwise directed.
32.2 km	Junction, with a bridge over the Wild Horse River. Good opportunity to fill up on water. Keep straight on Wildhorse Forest Service Road.
35 km	Cross a small bridge over to the east side of the valley. In 600 m, at a fork, keep left.

39.5 km	Keep left at a fork, then left again in 650 m across the Wild Horse River. There's a private cabin on the hill to your left. Keep climbing up rougher OHV track.
42.7 km	Avalanche debris across the path. Good panoramic view of the valley.
44.3 km	Top out at 1946 m on Wildhorse Ridge. The Top of the World Provincial Park boundary runs along the ridge to the west. The next 33 km are downhill. Keep checking your GPS, as there are a few gravel offshoots.
47.9 km	Turn right, heading downhill.
49.5 km	Continue on around a sharp right curve. It is easy to get sucked into following animal tracks that continue straight. The path travels downward across a drainage.
52.1 km	Sharp left curve, heading back across the drainage. The more established Lussier Forest Service Road begins on the other side. Mileage markers are present.
56.1 km	Top of the World Provincial Park trailhead on your right. Wilderness camping is permitted in the area.
78.2 km	Bridge over Coyote Creek. On the other side, keep left, heading uphill.
86.6 km	Drop down to Whiteswan Lake Forest Service Road. Alces Lake Campground is immediately ahead. $23/night for cycle-in sites, available on a first-come basis. Once settled, head back out to the main road and turn right. The primitive Lussier Hot Springs is 3.5 km to the west. Lock your bike to the chain-link fence and change in the outhouse. Temperatures for the springs vary throughout the season. The much cooler Lussier River runs adjacent. Hot or cold, it's a good chance to relax your muscles!

Day 2: Whiteswan Lake to Fernie (103 km)

Today's route heads back south along a parallel series of valleys.

Keep an eye out for the Sulphur Creek junction at 77 km. The first scouting mission sucked me into a downhill trance (and I raced an hour past it). The thought of grinding back uphill wasn't so appealing at the time, so I continued south to the end of the Bull River valley. Of course, this meant I would have to go back and scout the missing Fernie link later. Unfortunately, the narrow path up the mountain was blocked by precarious fog when I tried to drive it a month later. "Noooope!" my wife and co-pilot cringed. It wasn't until a year later that I would see Hartley Pass in all its gravel-grinding glory.

0 km	Head east on Whiteswan Lake Forest Service Road.
7.5 km	Pass Inlet Creek Campground at the far end of Whiteswan Lake. Turn right on the first unsigned gravel road, 400 m ahead. GPS is your friend once again today.
9.5 km	Keep left up the more established service road. Begin a gradual 5-km climb. A little confusing, with more-primitive forest tracks branching off at first (all of them dead end fairly quickly). The forestry footprint is very evident in the hills today.
14 km	Begin your descent, continuing to curve around to the Bull River valley.
18.8 km	The trail crosses a partially washed-out bridge over the Bull River (from June 2013 floods). Expect a few more ahead. Nothing major, just be careful of your footing. You are now on the east side of valley, heading south. Start a gradual 20-km climb.
22.8 km	At a path heading down across river, keep straight.
35.3 km	Begin an easy switchback climb to an unnamed pass at 1763 m. Top out in 3 km and begin a 39-km descent on what is now Queen Creek Road. Keep an eye out for trucks not expecting to see cyclists.
65.2 km	Cross a bridge and turn right on what is now Bull River Forest Service Road. 40 Mile Camp is here.
74.5 km	Fork left onto a track heading up to Sulphur Creek Road. Careful not to get sucked into the downhill continuation of Bull River Creek Road. Begin a 14-km climb up to Hartley Lake.
76.5 km	Sulphur Creek Campground is on the right.
88.4 km	Top out at an elevation of 1528 m. Hartley Lake Campground is 200 m off route. Keeping straight, begin an 8-km descent into the Elk Valley. Watch your speed on narrow Hartley Lake Road.
96.7 km	Turn right on paved Dicken Road. Enter residential area.
100.8 km	Turn left at a stop sign, then right onto Crowsnest Highway. Fernie Visitor Centre is on the corner. Open 9:00 a.m. to 5:00 p.m. Monday through Saturday.
101.8 km	Cross a bridge over Elk River and enter the city of Fernie. Turn left on 9 Avenue (into a shopping plaza) in 400 m.

Fernie is a full-service ski and mountain bike destination. Learn more at tourismfernie.com. With the Fernie RV Resort located at the north end of town (away from the pub hub), I would focus my energy on getting groceries in the plaza and then checking in at my site before dark.

Brew-to-go   Fernie Mountain Spirits is open 9:00 a.m. to 11:00 p.m. daily (ferniemountainspirits.com).

Restock   Kevin's Your Independent Grocer is open 8:00 a.m. to 10:00 p.m. daily. There is also a McDonald's, Tim Hortons and Starbucks in the on route plaza.

* Additional Fernie recommendations can be found in the Flathead Valley route.

102.4 km   At the north end of the plaza, turn right on 19 Street. Then, in 200 m, take your next left on the gravel 6 Avenue.

103.2 km   The Fernie RV Resort is 500 m ahead on your left. Thirteen tent sites, $42/night during the high season. This is your only established camping option within a reasonable distance from town. Water, WiFi, laundry and showers. Book in advance at ferniervresort.com.

Day 3: Fernie to Kikomun Creek (95 km)

Reward to anyone who finds my SPOT tracker. It rattled loose somewhere around the 53-km point on today's remote skirt of the Flathead Valley.

October 7, 2016. It was one of those days: a bout of unexpected snow and an onslaught of hypothermic climbs to contend with. My brake pads rubbed as a result, and the hot metal plates smoked as I doused them with water. A good reminder to carry at least one extra set of pads in mountainous regions.

Java fix   Big Bang Bagels (bigbangbagels.ca) is on route at 502 2 Avenue. Open 7:00 a.m. to 5:00 p.m. daily. Check out

their Mt. Fernie bagel: fried egg, aged white cheddar, avocado, tomato, grilled onion and your choice of ham, bacon or spinach and sprouts. Coffee roasted by Cuppers in Lethbridge.

Tune up A few blocks down, GearHub Sports (gearhub.ca) is at 401 1 Avenue. Of the three shops in the vicinity, GearHub is the first to open, at 8:30 a.m. The other two mosey in at 10:00.

0 km	Exit the campground and backtrack along 6 Avenue.
1 km	Turn left on 13 Street, then right on 2 Avenue in 500 m. Toward the end of the historic downtown, turn left on 4 Street and cross railroad tracks. Following that, turn right on Pine Avenue. The Fernie Aquatic Centre is on your left. There's a bike wash station at the jump park.
3 km	Turn left on Coal Creek Road. Follow straight through a residential area and onto gravel, now called the Fernie Coal Road. Begin gradual 21-km ascent. Keep straight unless otherwise directed.
6.2 km	There's a rifle range on your left.
8.4 km	Keep right where an unsigned road branches left. The original Coal Creek townsite was on the opposite side of the creek.
14.6 km	Begin a switchback up to the ridgeline.
17.8 km	Keep right at unsigned Coal Creek Forest Service Road junction.

27.7 km	Keep left on unsigned McEvoy Creek Forest Service Road.
33.1 km	Bottom out. Turn right up an unsigned service road through the cutline. The trail will soon duck left into trees on an "easier" route up the hill, the first of many times this forest service road will do this. Continue to follow these detours unless otherwise directed. Check your GPS if unsure.
35.2 km	Turn left down a detour. Expect to hike most of the next 3 km, both down and up, especially in muddy conditions (upwards of a 20 per cent gradient).
38.3 km	Emerge back into the cutline. Another quick descent ahead, followed by a more rideable 200-m climb.
42.7 km	Keep straight at a detour that heads to the right, uphill. The road bends around to the left on a short descent. Final push up to the ridgeline in 1 km.
44 km	The climb tops out at 1991 m. Flathead Peak is along the ridge to your left. Check your brakes! Begin the steep 9-km descent to the valley floor.
52.7 km	Turn right at a T-junction for Lodgepole Forest Service Road. Next, take a left on Wigwam Forest Service Road in 300 m. Begin gradual descent west through the Wigwam River valley.
56.1 km	Where the road bends, continue straight on a narrower path along the river bench. You have gone too far if you cross the river.
61.5 km	Fork right, heading up a short climb. Left drops down to the river. You should be back in cell service within the next 4 km.
69.4 km	Begin up a tighter section along the Wigwam River bench. The Elko sawmill soon becomes visible on the opposite side.
74 km	Trailhead junction. Turn left on River Forest Service Road, heading west across the Elk River. Turn right on Cascade Street at the top of a hill (entering Elko residential area), then right on Main, then left on Bate Avenue.
75.6 km	Turn left on Highway 93, heading downhill. On the left side of the road, in 650 m, just past a concrete barrier, look for a gravel two-track, part of The Great Trail (also known as the Trans Canada Trail). Turn left and begin a grassland route to Baynes Lake.

SOUTH COUNTRY RESTAURANT

Before heading downhill on Highway 93, look for a building 180 m
north with a bold store sign. This is the South Country Restaurant
and convenience store. Open 7:00 a.m. to 7:00 p.m., Monday
through Saturday.

78 km	Turn right on more established gravel road, then a quick right back onto trail.
79.4 km	Turn right, up a cutline, then quickly left back into the trees.
80.1 km	Turn right on a wider gravel road. Fork left in 300 m.
80.9 km	Turn left, back onto single track paralleling Highway 93.
83.1 km	Turn right on faint track through a hydro corridor. Exit the gate and safely cross the highway. Continue straight on a wider gravel road ahead.
85.1 km	Turn left at a T-junction. Fussee Lake is ahead.
89.2 km	Fork left, then left again onto Baynes Lake Dump Road.
91.5 km	Continue across Jaffray Baynes Lake Road, then right on Jaffray Baynes Lake Road North in 300 m.

SWEET ROAD

Looking for a snack or convenience-store item before settling in
for the night? Turn left on Jaffray Baynes Lake Road, then left on
Sweet Road. The Baynes Lake General Store is 1.5 km off route.
Open 11:00 a.m. to 7:00 p.m. daily.

92.3 km	Road ends. Continue straight along a narrower trail that bisects Baynes Lake. Keep an eye on your GPS, as there are a few gated trails in the area.
93.4 km	Fork right toward Surveyors Lake. In 800 m, enter the back side of a campground and continue through it to the trail kiosk on Kerr Road.

| 95.6 km | Kikomun Creek Provincial Park / Surveyors Lake Campground. Open early May to the end of September. Sites can be booked in advance at discovercamping.ca. $35/night plus reservation fee. After checking in, loosen your joints with a quick dip in Surveyors Lake. Grab a hot shower afterward. |

Day 4: Kikomun Creek to Cranbrook (62 km)

My first scout continued up the Kootenay River along The Great Trail (Trans Canada Trail). I would have preferred to take you this way in this guide but found the navigation quite convoluted. Combined with the tail end of yesterday's ride, the experience reinforced that much of the "Great Trail" still requires a GPS to adequately navigate. My chosen track is a more straightforward gravel grind around Mount Baker.

| 0 km | Turn left out of the campground along Kikomun Newgate Road. |
| 2.3 km | Cross a bridge over the Kootenay River. |

LAKE KOOCANUSA

Lake Koocanusa Campsite & Marina is on your left, just across the bridge (koocanusa.wordpress.com). The camp store is open 9:00 a.m. to 7:00 p.m. daily during the summer. Last chance for food until Cranbrook.

5.2 km	Keep right on Caven Creek Forest Service Road. Surface soon turns to gravel.
11 km	Keep left at a fork with a wooden sign pointing to Wardner. To the right is where The Great Trail (Trans Canada Trail) starts to get messy. Continue uphill.
19.2 km	Turn right on Gold Creek Road. A yellow radio communication sign at the junction confirms the correct route. Gradual 24-km ascent ahead.

22.3 km	St. Louis camping area is on your right.
26.6 km	Cross Gold Creek.
38.2 km	Cross Gold Creek a second time.
39.7 km	And a third time.
42.6 km	Begin the lengthy descent into Cranbrook.
49.8 km	Phillips Reservoir is on your right.
53.8 km	At an intersection with 30 Avenue, keep left. The Gold Creek convenience store is on the corner. Gold Creek becomes 21 Street South.
55 km	Turn right on 20 Avenue, left on 17 Street, and right on 14 Avenue. Downtown is 2.2 km ahead on Baker Street. Best to stop here unless you want to complete the full loop back to the Visitor Centre.

CRANBROOK RECOMMENDATIONS

Foood! The Heid Out Restaurant & Brewhouse (theheidout.ca) is at 821 Baker Street. After a greasy meal, grab a growler from Fisher Peak Brewing Company, crafted on site. They close at 10:00 p.m. Monday through Wednesday; 11:00 p.m. on Thursday; 12:00 a.m. on Friday and Saturday; and 9:00 p.m. on Sunday. Rated #2 on TripAdvisor.

58.2 km	Turn right on 2 Street North, then left on Victoria Avenue in 700 m.
60 km	Cross Highway 3/95 and continue straight on Theatre Road.
61.1 km	Turn right on McPhee Road.
61.9 km	Finish back at the Visitor Centre.

WILDHORSE CYCLING CLUB

Got an extra day? There is a good network of trails along the slope leading back into town. Connect with the Wildhorse Cycling Club (bikewildhorse.ca) for maps and local intel.

EXPERT ROUTES

---

*Are you a proficient cyclist
and outdoors person?*

*Have you completed all routes in the
book leading up to this point?*

*Is the word "suffer" an integral
part of your lexicon?*

Enter the path less travelled.

8. FLATHEAD VALLEY

START AND FINISH   Fernie, British Columbia

WHO SHOULD RIDE?   Sure to test your grit, the Flathead Valley includes a challenging single-track section to Sparwood, three arduous mountain passes, the trepidation you feel while travelling through a region known as the "Grizzly Bear Highway," and one of the toughest hike-a-bike sections of any route. The Flathead Valley is a mandatory primer for anyone interested in taking on the full Great Divide Mountain Bike Route.

DISTANCE   292 km

ELEVATION GAIN   3783 m

SUGGESTED NUMBER OF DAYS   4

About the Route

The consensus among Divide riders is that if you can make it through Alberta, British Columbia and Montana, you will likely endure to Antelope Wells. That first week teaches you a lot about how your body and bike will hold up. The technical piece of the equation (types of trails to expect, the severity of climbs, the remoteness), however, can be answered by completing just one section: this trip in the Flathead Valley, southwest British Columbia.

This wildlife corridor carries a certain mystique in race lore. Toward the end of Day 1 — for lead riders — just as you are leaving Sparwood (your next restock is 200 km ahead in Montana), you get the sense that something heavy is about to set in. You may also start to feel apprehensive about the unknowns of remote travel at nightfall.

ELEVATION PROFILE

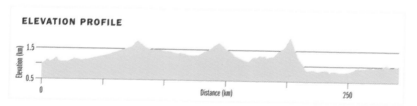

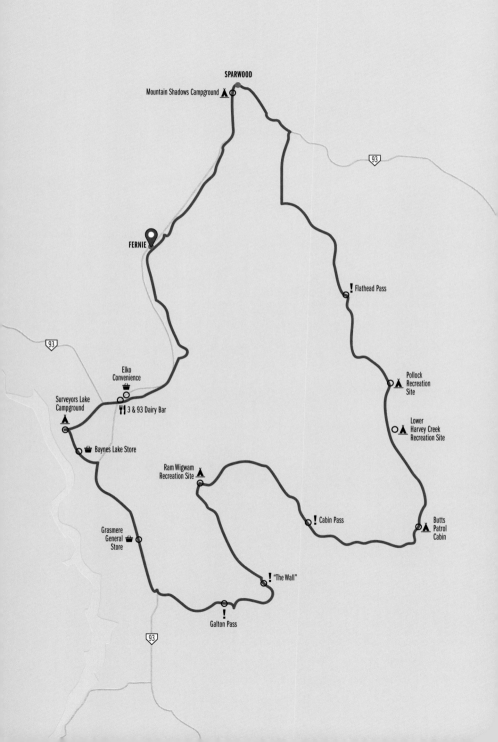

SPARWOOD

Mountain Shadows Campground

FERNIE

93

Flathead Pass

93

Elko
Convenience

Surveyors Lake
Campground

3 & 93 Dairy Bar

Pollock
Recreation
Site

Lower
Harvey Creek
Recreation Site

Baynes Lake Store

Ram Wigwam
Recreation Site

Cabin Pass

Butts
Patrol
Cabin

Grasmere
General
Store

"The Wall"

Galton Pass

93

Keep a diligent watch for wildlife and make noise as you climb up and over Flathead Pass (into the backcountry), followed by Cabin Pass, then up and over the epic Galton Pass (back into the front country).

Getting to Fernie The nearest international airport is in Calgary, 313 km (3.5 hours) northeast of Fernie. The Fernie Shuttle (thefernieshuttle.com) offers direct transportation for $240/adult for a return ticket. If driving your own car, check in with a local hotel about parking for a few days.

Trail improvements Contact the Fernie Trails Alliance (fernietrailsalliance.com) to check on the status of the Elk Valley Trail.

U.S. border Although Flathead River Road continues south from Butts Patrol Cabin on Day 3, wandering into the u.s. (and Glacier National Park) is strictly prohibited. The nearest legal crossing is at Roosville, Montana. Google "Flathead border feast" for a better (albeit cheeky) understanding of the border region.

Day 1: Fernie to Sparwood (32 km)

Officially opened in 2004, Coal Discovery Trail is a tremendous Elk Valley link. Just keep in mind that what looks like a two- to three-hour jaunt will likely take most touring riders twice that. We experienced this first-hand on our supported tour. The trail is still fairly rough around the edges. There is a random spattering of trail blazes, overgrown sections, easy-to-miss links that weave in and out of a cutline, and a healthy dose of pitchy climbs. Consider it a warm-up for the mountain passes ahead.

An old coal-mining town that has evolved into a four-season tourism hub, Fernie takes great pride in its trail network and multi-day mountain bike events such as TransRockies and the Fernie 3. All services are here. Learn more at tourismfernie.com.

FERNIE RECOMMENDATIONS

Java fix One of my favourite homemade breakfast stops is Freshies (freshiesfernie.com). "Great coffee and crepes" is their motto. Open 5:00 a.m. to 5:00 p.m. during the week; 6:00 a.m. to 5:00 p.m. on the weekend. Located at 632 2 Avenue.

Sleep on the cheap The Fernie RV Resort (ferniervresort.com) is the closest campsite, at $42/night during July and August. For indoor accommodations, check out the Raging Elk Hostel (ragingelk.com). $32/night for Hostelling International (HI) members. The Snow Valley Motel is another value option, and it has free fat bike rentals for guests!

Stock up Save-On-Foods is at 792 2 Avenue (near all the coffee and bike shops). Open 8:00 a.m. to 9:00 p.m. daily. Closer to the Fernie RV Resort at the north end of town, Kevin's Your Independent Grocer is open 8:00 a.m. to 10:00 p.m. daily.

Tune up There are three shops located within a few blocks of 2 Avenue. GearHub Sports (gearhub.ca), open 10:00 a.m. to 8:00 p.m. daily. Ski Base (skibase.com), open 10:00 a.m. to 6:00 p.m. daily. Straight Line Bicycle & Skis (shop.straightlinefernie.com), open same hours. All are accustomed to dealing with mountain bikes. Hours vary seasonally.

0 km	Begin on the main street, corner of 2 Avenue and 4 Street. Head west one block, cross the train tracks, then go left on Pine Avenue. Merge onto the signed Coal Discovery Trail / Trans Canada Trail, heading north into the trees. Pay close attention to your GPS from here until Sparwood. The route will become progressively more difficult to follow.
1.2 km	Cross Ridgemont Avenue. Keep right at the next two forks. Ridgemont Drive runs parallel for a few kilometres.
3.5 km	Coal Discovery Trail kicks up the ridge through an engaging network of Fernie single track. Weaving in and out of a cutline, you find yourself amongst a handful of not-so-obvious intersections. Catch your breath and look for the next trail blaze.
14.4 km	Unsigned intersection. Left heads west to the small town of Hosmer (no services) along Highway 3. Not far ahead on the right are the graffitied ruins of a coal-oven. Continue straight along the cutline. Sparwood is responsible for this end of the trail.
20.9 km	Loop around the Wilson Lake gravel quarry on your left.
32.2 km	Turn left onto unsigned road. Mountain Shadows Campground (mountainshadows.ca) is just ahead on your right. Hot showers and firewood; $25–$35/night. Book in advance by email to stay@mountainshadows.ca. Do not expect a quick response in the off season.

SPARWOOD RECOMMENDATIONS (EVENING)

Most services are 2 km north of the campground along Highway 3. Keep an eye out for one of the world's largest dump trucks, the green "Titan," located within a block of the Sparwood Visitor Centre (open 9:00 a.m. to 5:00 p.m. daily). Coal mine tours are also available. More information at sparwood.ca.

Brew   Silver Fox Neighbourhood Pub is adjacent to the campground on the west side of Highway 93. It serves typical pub fare.

Greasy spoon   The A&W at 131 Aspen Drive is a staple for Divide riders. This is their last warm meal until Eureka, Montana. If you are looking for more local flavour, check out Funky Pizza at 113 Centennial Square. Open daily until 9:00 p.m.

Restock   Within the same few blocks, you can find Overwaitea Foods and the Husky gas station. The latter is my preference for bike visibility. It is next door to the A&W, which makes for a quick 1-2 stop.

Sleep in the heat   The Causeway Bay Hotel (causewaybayhotels. ca/sparwood.html) is another popular spot for Divide riders in inclement weather. ~$100 for a room.

Day 2: Sparwood to Flathead Valley (91 km)

The first of three big mountain passes begins at the ghost town of Corbin. On the 2012 Tour Divide, I became hopelessly lost while riding through in the middle of the night (again ending up on private mine property). Knowing how to use your GPS before you take on *any* of the prescribed routes is essential. Now enter the Flathead Valley.

0 km	Heading back out of the campground, turn right on Highway 3. You are on paved false flat for the next 36 km.
1.5 km	Turn left on Red Cedar, then left on Aspen. There are Sparwood services along this stretch. Last chance to stock up for the next 191 km (almost two full days).
2.2 km	Turn right on Elk Highway, then left back onto Highway 3.
13.9 km	Turn right on Corbin Road, heading south.
36.8 km	The road bends to the right at the entrance to Teck's Coal Mountain operations. There are a few dilapidated mining homes (possible emergency shelters) interspersed amongst current dwellings. The gravel Flathead Valley Forest Service Road forks off to the right in 400 m. There is signage at trailhead.
37 km	Begin the more obvious climb up Flathead Pass. Terraced Coal Mountain is on your left (on other side of fence). Raw materials extracted here are used in the production of steel. Teck announced in 2016 that the mine would be closed and returned to public stakeholders in late 2017. My 2012 lost wander was up this mountain.
46.4 km	Top out at an elevation of 1775 m. Expect a myriad of possible conditions on the descent: water flowing down across the trail,

snowy embankments, no discernible path. "Choose your own adventure" down this drainage.

55.1 km   Keep left at what feels like the bottom of the pass (still a net downhill to Butts Patrol Cabin). Right follows McLatchie Forest Service Road. Test out your vocal cords and start to make noise as you enter a meadow.

58.1 km   Keep right. The trail continues to follow the Flathead River (also known as the North Fork) southward along an embankment.

65.5 km   Cross a bridge over the Flathead River. Pollock Creek camping area is just ahead. You are now on the west side of the valley.

73.9 km   Lower Harvey Creek camping area is left. Just ahead, keep straight at intersection for Lodgepole Forest Service Road.

90.2 km   Keep straight at a junction for Kishinea Forest Service Road. Left heads over the Flathead River and connects with our Castle route.

90.9 km   Butts Patrol Cabin is on your right. The site is composed of a few dilapidated shelters. First-come basis for backcountry folk. The frontrunners of the Tour Divide try to make it here on their first night out, which makes for a 320-km opening push from Banff! Commerce Creek is nearby.

Day 3: Flathead Valley to Kikomun Creek (124 km)

I last ventured up Cabin Pass on Day 2 of the Tour Divide in 2015. After only a few hours of rest (at Butts Patrol Cabin), our lead group pushed on, wearily weaving up the first few pitches by headlamp — my watch read 3:15 a.m. Should you also feel a little groggy, the subsequent 16-km descent is sure to kickstart your senses, and just in time to begin the next lengthy climb up Galton Pass.

0 km	Continue south along Flathead Valley Road.
2.3 km	Turn right and go up the unsigned Cabin Forest Service Road. Then right again at a fork through a cutline in 800 m.
4.4 km	Cross a bridge over Howell Creek. You might want to fill your water bottles here. Ahead is a steep 200-m push, the start of a 16-km climb up Cabin Pass.
21.7 km	Top out at an elevation of 1728 m. Look for a creek flowing on your left as the trail plateaus. A lengthy descent begins shortly.
45.2 km	Bottom out. Turn left on Wigwam Forest Service Road, dropping down across a bridge. Ram–Wigwam Campground is here.
46.1 km	At a gated road, keep right. Cross the Wigwam River and begin a 3-km climb up a rolling river bench.
65.8 km	Turn right at a small rock cairn for an overgrown single track. You have gone too far if you cross back over the Wigwam River.
66.9 km	Begin a steep hike-a-bike up "The Wall." You might need to take your packs off and make several trips, especially in wet conditions. This challenging track exits onto a plateau in 400 m, following a meadow of young trees. The more established Phillips Forest Service Road is ahead.
71.2 km	After short dip at the south end of the mountain, begin the final 8-km climb up Galton Pass.
77 km	Switchback right, heading up a steeper pitch.
79.6 km	Top out at an elevation of 1889 m. Begin a 16-km descent into the front country. Keep an eye out for trucks coming up the narrow road.
83.7 km	Continue descending along what is known as Connor Road. The u.s. border is less than 600 m south from this point.
90.4 km	Reach a corner overlooking the Tobacco Plains, home to a Ktunaxa Nation community (ktunaxa.org). First Nations cultivated tobacco in the meadows in this region until 1710. Continue descending around a switchback.

92.5 km	Turn right onto Highway 93. Left takes you to the U.S. border at Roosville. Here the Great Divide Mountain Bike Route continues south through Montana. Tempted?
100.7 km	Hamlet of Grasmere.

GRASMERE GENERAL STORE

Restock Grasmere General Store is on your left, open 9:00 a.m. to 7:00 p.m. Monday through Friday and 10:00 a.m. to 7:00 p.m. Saturday. There are a few campsites in the area if you need to stop early. Ask at the store for details.

110.3 km	Highway drops to a bridge over the Elk River.
115.4 km	Turn left on Jaffray Baynes Lake Road. Keep an eye out for white-tailed deer leaping through the knee-high grass and ponderosa pine.
119.1 km	Turn right on Sweet Road and enter the community of Baynes Lake. Approximately 160 seasonal residences.

SWEET ROAD

Foood! The Baynes Lake General Store is 1.5 km off route. Open 11:00 a.m. to 7:00 p.m. daily.

119.9 km	Turn right, back onto Jaffray Baynes Lake Road. No painted shoulder.
123.5 km	Turn left on Kikomun Road.
124 km	Turn left into Kikomun Creek Provincial Park / Surveyors Lake Campground. Open early May to the end of September. Sites can be booked up to five months in advance at discovercamping.ca. $35/night plus reservation free. Hot showers included.

Day 4: Kikomun Creek to Fernie (45 km)

Take the morning to relax! If the weather is agreeable, head down and take a dip in Surveyors Lake. You can access the water via an embankment at the south end of the campground. Painted turtles make their home here (please do not disturb). Plan for a 10:00 a.m. or later departure to take advantage of the dairy bar up the road. Just don't stuff your face. The gravel grind along the river valley from Elko to Fernie still has a few cramp-inducing pitches.

0 km	Exiting the campground, turn right, onto Kikomun Road. There is no painted shoulder.
7.6 km	Turn right on Highway 3. Now there's a shoulder.
9.9 km	Keep straight at the junction with Highway 93.

3 & 93

Foood! The 3 & 93 Dairy Bar (dairybar.ca) and picnic area is on your left. An iconic local destination that has been in business since 1964. Generally open 11:00 a.m. to 8:00 p.m. early May through mid-September. How about a garlic mozza bacon burger? Some pickle fries? Or maybe a nut-buster parfait to recoup some of those lost calories?

11.1 km	Near the top of a hill, turn right on Bate Avenue into the small sawmill town of Elko. Head east three blocks and fork right on Main Street. In another three blocks, fork left on Cascade Street.

SOUTH COUNTRY RESTAURANT AND STORE

Restock Continue past Bate Avenue across the bridge on Highway 93. Look for building 100 m ahead on your left with a bold store sign. This is the South Country Restaurant and convenience store, open 7:00 a.m. to 7:00 p.m. Monday through Saturday.

12.1 km	Turn left down River Forest Service Road. Cross a bridge over the Elk River, which you parallel north to Fernie. Keep checking your GPS, as there are numerous gravel offshoots.

26 km	There's a hydro corridor immediately ahead of you. Take the left fork for Lodgepole Forest Service Road.
27.1 km	At a stop sign junction on Cokato Road, turn left. The road leading straight has a yellow sign reading "Must call to 17.5 km and up."
30.1 km	At a yellow 20 km sign, keep north across a cattle guard. You may see signs for The Great Trail (Trans Canada Trail). Possibly still work to be completed. Left is a possible detour to Highway 93 via the ghost town of Morrissey. The riverside site served as a First World War internment camp between 1915 and 1918. Learn more at the museum in Fernie.
38.4 km	Cokato Road turns to asphalt.
43.8 km	Cross Coal Creek and continue straight on what is now Pine Avenue. A few blocks ahead on your right is the Fernie Aquatic Centre.
44.5 km	Turn left on Ridgemont Drive and finish in downtown Fernie.

TRAIL TO ALE CHALLENGE

Energy to burn? Ride 2 km north to the Fernie Brewing Co. (ferniebrewing.com) and take on its "Trail to Ale" challenge. You will be tasked with bagging three local peaks within a 24-hour period, covering 45 km and 1200 m of climbing. A free cold beer and a medal await the victor.

9. THREE POINT

START AND FINISH   Bragg Creek, Alberta

WHO SHOULD RIDE?   Due to flood damage along a great majority of the Kananaskis Trail system, my 2016 scout of Three Point could largely be considered a hiking/bushwhacking/orienteering route with some biking thrown into the mix. Trail improvements are in the works or have now been completed.

DISTANCE   173 km

ELEVATION GAIN   3616 m

SUGGESTED NUMBER OF DAYS   3

About the Route

Caught in the grasp of a yet another soul-crushing hike-a-bike, pushing through overgrowth and mud, I would often wonder, *Is this too much?*

Comparing the flood-ravaged Kananaskis to my experience along the often unrideable Arizona Trail (part of the bikepacking triple crown in the u.s.), it dawned on me that I might still need to shed some of my groomed sensibilities.

The veteran bikepacking crew have come to appreciate that not every trail will flow with ease. And an unrideable track may in fact be a doorway into more explorative instincts. So, I say, "Hike, on!" There are tremendous panoramic views atop Jumpingpound Ridge, quaint meadows around Threepoint Mountain and inspiring black shale cliffs heading down Gorge Creek.

Along the way, expect to encounter horseback riders who can still navigate the carnage with relative ease. You're in cowboy country, partner!

ELEVATION PROFILE

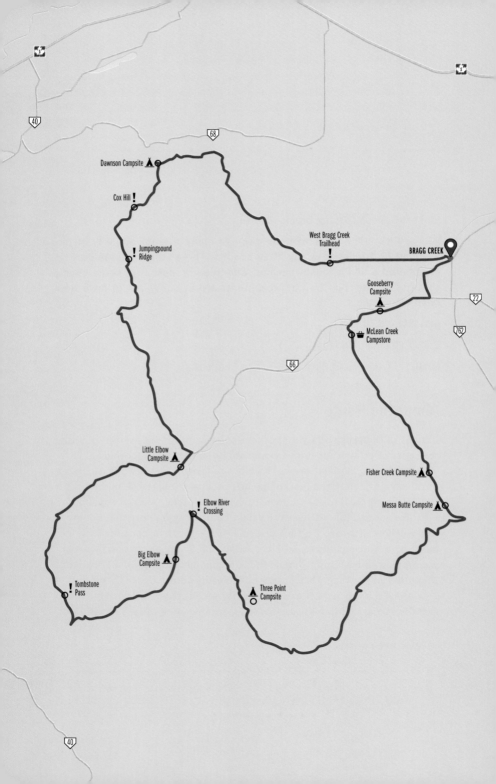

Best time to go Low-lying water and creek crossing will be unnecessarily difficult during the spring runoff from the mountains. Ware Creek Trail and McLean Creek Trail are also closed December to May. I suggest heading out between July and September.

Getting to Bragg Creek Bragg Creek is 45 km west of downtown Calgary. There is no bus service. Park in town or ride in from Calgary. Roadies frequent the out-and-back route along Highway 8 on weekends.

Trail improvements Keep a close eye on the restoration efforts of local groups such as the Bragg Creek Trails Association, the Calgary Mountain Bike Alliance and the Friends of Kananaskis. Also Alberta Parks.

The more remote southern sections (toward the Sheep River valley) will likely remain status quo for the foreseeable future.

Day 1: Bragg Creek to Dawson (31 km)

West Bragg Creek is a popular launching point for Calgary and area mountain bikers.

My introduction to these trails was during the infamous Bow 80 event in September 2009. It was the last year that Bow Cycle organized this 80-km epic through Kananaskis. Hypothermic conditions along the high ridges of Jumpingpound and Cox Hill were at first to blame (there was a mandatory check-in with paramedics when you crossed the finish). The odds of ever bringing the event back were then eviscerated by the June 2013 floods.

Tom Snow (part of The Great Trail, also known as the Trans Canada Trail) bore the brunt of the route's damage. And I'll be honest, as a cross-country race route, this is a search-and-rescue operation waiting to happen. But as an expert bikepacking route, with GPS in hand, extra food, and tempered expectations, it is very much a character-building experience.

Check trail updates before heading out.

BRAGG CREEK RECOMMENDATIONS

Bragg Creek is your one reliable service option en route (pack enough for four days). All stores are centrally located around the Bragg Creek Shopping Centre plaza. Learn more at visitbraggcreek.com.

Java fix There are three grab-and-go options. The Heart of Bragg Creek (theheartofbraggcreek.com), Bragg Creek Café & Baking Co. (braggcreekcafe.com) and Cinnamon Spoon, a traditional stop for cyclists riding out from Calgary.

Sleep on the cheap There are no hostels or campgrounds right in town. Ironically, the first youth hostel in North America was erected along White Avenue in 1933. It is now the site of Scoops & Snacks ice-cream shop. Expect to pay $200+ for B&B style accommodations in the area. The closest campground is Gooseberry, 8 km southwest of town. Book in advance at albertaparks.ca.

Stock up Bragg Creek Family Foods is open 8:00 a.m. to 8:00 p.m. daily. Also nearby are a Shell convenience store and a Subway.

Tune up Calgary Cycle/Cycle 22x (calgarycycle.com/locations /22x) is well-versed in mountain bikes.

0 km	Begin from the Bragg Creek Shopping Centre. Head west on Balsam Avenue. In 400 m, cross the Elbow River, then turn left at a T-junction for Wintergreen Road. Continue along what is now West Bragg Creek Road.
9.5 km	West Bragg Creek Day Use parking area is on your right. Several cross-country ski, mountain bike and hiking trails branch off from here. Keep straight on gravel Mountain Road.
11.3 km	Turn right on Moose Connector, then right again on Moose Loop in 600 m.
12.1 km	Turn left on Moose Loop, heading across the creek.
14.1 km	Turn right up Tom Snow. When scouted in 2016 the field ahead was overgrown, with no discernible trail. Check your GPS and pick the track that works best for you. If hiking, follow the rule of Scottish mountaineer William W. Naismith: allow 1 hour for every 5 km forward, plus 1 hour for every 600 m of ascent.
19.0 km	Continue on to recently rebuilt trail and keep going straight.
25 km	Cross the Moose Creek Connector trail.
25.3 km	Slight right onto gravel road.
25.8 km	Turn left onto Tom Snow Trail.
30.8 km	Turn right to follow trail to a campground. Straight continues up Cox Hill and across a fairly new bridge over Jumpingpound Creek.

PHOTO: MATTHEW CLARK

| 31.4 km | Dawson Equestrian Campground along Powderface Trail (road). There are five walk-in campsites for $26/night plus $12 reservation fee. Water pump, fire pits and pit toilets available. Book in advance at albertaparks.ca. |

Day 2: Dawson to Big Elbow (68 km)

Begin your day with two solid climbs up Cox Hill and Jumpingpound Ridge. When the weather is favourable, you see some tremendous views of the Front Range. Descending to Little Elbow Campground, you have the optional challenge of a climb up Tombstone Pass. Expect some washouts and chunky rock. No bushwhacking today.

0 km	Backtrack 500 m across Jumpingpound Creek to the Tom Snow junction. Turn right and begin a steady 5-km climb up Cox Hill Trail. Hike-a-bike for those carrying a heavier load. Keep an eye out for riders bombing down.
6.3 km	Top out at an elevation of 2191 m. Begin descent in 100 m.
8.5 km	Bottom out and begin the 4-km climb up to Jumpingpound Ridge
9.3 km	Turn right at a T-junction for Jumpingpound Ridge Trail.
12.3 km	Top out an elevation of 2192 m. Enjoy the great panoramic views before beginning a steeper descent out of the alpine. Switchbacks ahead.
17.7 km	Bottom out in meadow. Turn right on an overgrown dirt road, then left on the gravel Powderface Trail in 650 m.
18.5 km	Cross a bridge over Canyon Creek and begin the first of several rolling gravel climbs.
23.7 km	Cross over a Prairie Creek culvert.
27.5 km	Top out and begin the 4-km descent.
33.2 km	Gravel turns into the asphalt Highway 66x. Turn right at a junction, continuing west. Forgetmenot Pond is ahead on your left.
34.8 km	Enter Little Elbow Campground. 30 walk-in sites at Loop C. $29/night plus $12 reservation fee. Pit toilets and water pump in the parking area. Book in advance at albertaparks.ca. If tired, consider stopping here for the night. Tombstone Pass is ahead.

SHORTCUT

You can avoid Tombstone Pass (the next 35 km) by following these cues:

0 km	Adjacent to Loop C in the campground, cross the Harold Chapman Suspension Bridge over the Little Elbow River. Turn right at the next two junctions and head southward down Big Elbow Trail. Navigate some washouts ahead.
8 km	Big Elbow Backcountry Campground is on the left. Details below.

36.2 km	Begin up Little Elbow Trail at the far end of the campground.
40.1 km	Bridge over Little Elbow River may be washed out.
46.5 km	Mount Romulus Backcountry Campground is on the right.
54.6 km	Top out at Tombstone Pass, elevation 2234 m. Begin descending.

| 56.8 km | Keep left down Little Elbow Trail. Track heading right leads to Tombstone Lakes (1.7-km hike. Bikes not permitted). Turn left again in 200 m, continuing down Big Elbow Trail. Tombstone Backcountry Campground is 200 m west, off route. |
| 68 km | Big Elbow Backcountry Campground is on the right. $12/night plus backcountry fee. Fire pits, food storage and pit toilets. Book in advance at albertaparks.ca. |

Day 3: Big Elbow to Bragg Creek (74 km)

After fording the Elbow River, climb steeply along a series of horse-trodden trails to the back side of Threepoint Mountain. After enjoying the meadow plateau for an hour or two, you are soon back on a muddled hiking/biking routine down the overgrown slopes of Gorge Creek. Make sure to give right of way to any horseback riders coming through (they will likely give further instruction).

From the Gorge Creek parking lot, I originally had to divert off-route to Turner Valley for a restock. It is very easy to underestimate the number of calories you will burn with all the hike-a-bike, both today and on Day 1. My second pass up Ware Creek Trail was surprisingly tranquil. The decommissioned road feels like an overgrown highway in a zombie apocalypse movie.

0 km	Continue northeast along Big Elbow Trail (backtracking if you took yesterday's shortcut).
4.8 km	Look for the faint Threepoint Mountain single track heading left through a patch of trees along the riverbank. There's a small trail sign at a junction that's easy to miss. In 400 m look for signal tape on the opposite side of the Elbow River. Figure out the best place to cross.
5.3 km	Begin up a steep embankment with deep horse tracks. It's a 2-km hike-a-bike to the ridgeline, part of Don Getty Wildland Provincial Park.
7.3 km	Attain the ridgeline and its great valley view. Keep an eye on your GPS, as the next meadow section is not well signed. Expect also to be on and off your bike quite a bit as you navigate small creek crossings, muddy horse tracks, exposed roots and random forks in the trail.
9.6 km	The path briefly dips east, heading across Threepoint Creek.
12.5 km	Cross Rock Creek to the opposite side of the meadow.
14 km	This is one of two intersecting paths heading down to the former Threepoint Backcountry Campground (1 km off route), which now accommodates random backcountry camping. Continue

straight along what is now Gorge Creek Trail. You soon find yourself on an exposed ridge overlooking the black shale slopes of Gorge Creek. Challenging hike-a-bike down.

15.9 km	Cross Gorge Creek. Expect overgrown trails as you head up the opposite side.
17.6 km	Keep straight at a junction for Blue Rock Creek Trail.
20.5 km	Keep straight at an intersection for South Gorge Creek Trail.
24.4 km	Turn right at a junction and continue east along Gorge Creek.
25.4 km	Gorge Creek parking lot. Exiting at the north end, continue left at junction with Range Road 55A. Head north through a gate onto decommissioned Ware Creek Trail. Watch for cattle for the next 11 km. There are also a few washed-out sections (legacy of the 2013 Sheep River flood).

TURNER VALLEY RESTOCK

If you have miscalculated your calories, you may want to consider riding 30 km off route to Turner Valley. Head south out of the parking lot, then east along paved Sheep River Road. In case of emergency, go to the Sheep River Park headquarters, roughly half that distance (they also have water). Once restocked, you can either double back or continue on asphalt to Millarville. From there, head west along Highway 549 to McLean Creek Road (rejoining the route at the 44-km mark). Additional options are listed in the sidebars below.

29.3 km	Link Creek Trail is on your left. A bridge ahead was washed away by flooding, but even if it's still out, it shouldn't be hard to navigate around.
35.7 km	Cross through a fence into Ware Creek Provincial Recreation Area. Continue north on more-established gravel road. Expect OHV traffic for the next 29 km.
42.5 km	Cross Threepoint Creek and turn left at an uphill intersection for McLean Creek Road. Wild camping allowed beyond 1 km of the road.

MILLARVILLE RESTOCK

Second-guessing your restock needs? At the intersection for McLean Creek Road, turn right and head 17 km off route (asphalt begins in 3 km) to the small village of Millarville. The general store (est. 1926) is open 8:00 a.m. to 6:00 p.m. Monday through Friday; 9:00 a.m. to 5:00 p.m. on Saturday; and 10:00 a.m. to 4:00 p.m. on Sunday.

44.6 km	Mesa Butte Provincial Recreation Area on left. Camping generally reserved for equestrian riders.
47.9 km	Fisher Creek Provincial Recreation Area and Campground. $29/night plus $12 reservation fee for walk-in campsites.

Water pump on site (you still want to treat). Book in advance at albertaparks.ca.

49.3 km	Turn right on Range Road 51A. Straight heads to a gated road.
61.5 km	Turn right on paved McLean Creek Road.

MCLEAN CREEK CAMPER CENTRE

McLean Creek Camper Centre is on the corner. Open May 1 to Canadian Thanksgiving (early October). Campsite, showers and small convenience items.

62.8 km	Turn right on Highway 66.
65.7 km	Elbow Valley Visitor Centre and Gooseberry Campground. Pay phone, free WiFi and washroom inside. Open mid-May. Closed during lunch hours. Gooseberry is the last camping opportunity before Bragg Creek. $29/night plus $12 reservation fee for walk-in sites. Book in advance at albertaparks.ca.
69.6 km	Turn left on Highway 758. Sign reads "Bragg Creek 3 km."
71.3 km	Enter Bragg Creek Provincial Park. Ride back up alongside the Elbow River and continue into town on what is now White Avenue.
74.4 km	Finish at Bragg Creek Village Centre.

BRAGG CREEK RECOMMENDATIONS

Foood! The Powderhorn Saloon (powderhornsaloon.ca) is a western-themed bar that has an appreciation for customers with a bit of dirt on their boots. Burgers and beer are the specialty. Open every day until "late."

Ice cream 76 flavours of ice cream at Frontier Candy, est. 1979, which is usually open around 11:00 a.m. and close at 6:00 p.m. during the week, a little later on Saturday and Sunday (weather dependent).

10. ICEFIELDS PARKWAY IN WINTER

START   Banff, Alberta

FINISH   Jasper, Alberta

WHO SHOULD RIDE?   Only those with winter-camping and fat-bike experience are encouraged to attempt the route. You also need to maintain a base level of fitness (and ability to sit on the saddle for long hours) through the off season.

DISTANCE   291 km

ELEVATION GAIN   +2836 m / –3163 m

SUGGESTED NUMBER OF DAYS   4

About the Route

Begin from Banff along the Bow Valley Parkway. This popular scenic detour (paralleling the Trans-Canada Highway) winds through a forest alley alongside the world-renowned Bow River, a tremendous four-season fly-fishing destination.

The route then kicks north from Lake Louise along the Icefields Parkway to Jasper. Consistently ranked one of Canada's most popular (summer) cycling routes, its attractions include Athabasca Falls, Sunwapta Falls, Columbia Icefield Discovery Centre, two big climbs of Sunwapta and Bow Pass, pristine lakes and waterways, imposing limestone cliffs near Big Bend, plenty of camping opportunities, hostels, full-service lodges and countless hiking trails that wend through Banff and Jasper national parks.

ELEVATION PROFILE

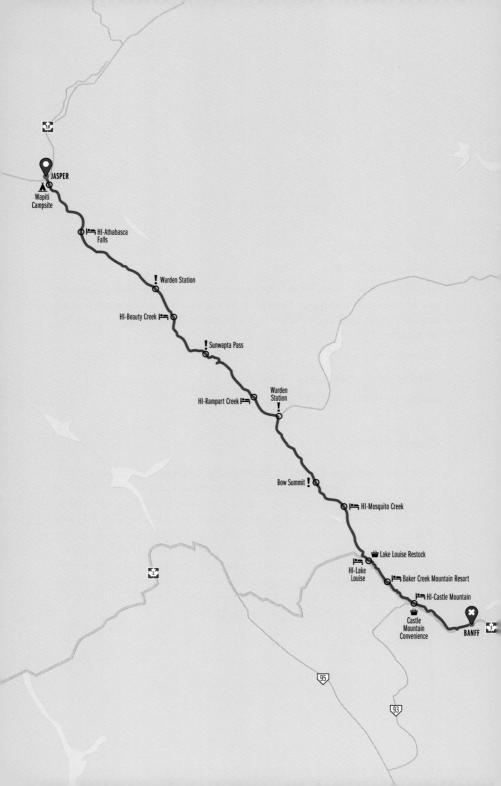

JASPER

Wapiti Campsite

HI-Athabasca Falls

Warden Station

HI-Beauty Creek

Sunwapta Pass

HI-Rampart Creek

Warden Station

Bow Summit

HI-Mosquito Creek

Lake Louise Restock

HI-Lake Louise

Baker Creek Mountain Resort

HI-Castle Mountain

Castle Mountain Convenience

BANFF

95

93

Shifting to winter, familiar asphalt is now transformed into compacted snow and ice bounded by fluffy high snowbanks, greatly reduced services and far less tourist traffic. Still, the parkway continues to be plowed, roadside phones carry a dial tone and the hostels stoke their wood stoves hourly. Winter hostelling is a cozy experience that only ice climbers, backcountry skiers and gaiter-equipped hikers seem to take advantage of. And, I say, why not us winter "fatpackers" too?

Many have asked about a hut-to-hut experience. The aforementioned roadside network is as close as you are going to get to that in the Canadian Rockies, especially in winter, as the alpine cabin experience is largely reserved for hikers. And as far as groomed through-routes of any consequence, the Icefields Parkway, much like Yukon's Dempster Highway, should very much be considered an accessible bucket-list adventure. Just the right amount of safety. Just the right amount of unknown. Consider it a new take on an old favourite.

If you only remember three points from here on, these are them:

1. You need to be 100 per cent self-sufficient once you leave Banff.
2. Plan for absolutely all conditions: snow, rain, ice, whiteout storms, freezing temperatures and extreme windchill, as well as the possibility of unseasonably warm conditions.
3. Budget at least four extra days for road closures and shuttling back to Banff. Your plans may change en route.

Bike of choice A fully rigid fat bike with studded tires is the best tool for the job. Fully kitted rentals (with bikepacking bags and Bar Mitts) can be arranged through Rebound Cycle in Canmore (reboundcycle.com), open 10:00 a.m. to 6:00 p.m. Monday through Saturday and 10:00 a.m. to 5:00 p.m. on Sunday.

Emergency shelter   *Plan A* Should you get caught out and not be able to make your reserved hostel in time, try snagging a last-minute room at another location. Managers are usually receptive. *Plan B* Hitchhike. *Plan C* Look for a rest stop with a covered washroom or picnic area, usually within proximity (please note that I am not advocating this as a legal camping option). *All Plans* Regardless, I highly encourage you to carry a winter sleeping bag and emergency bivouac or tent for peace of mind. If you reserve at Beauty Creek, you need a sleeping bag for sure. You also must sign a waiver by email to acknowledge that this is a rustic accommodation (you cannot just roll up without a reservation — the doors are locked). All other hostels have linens.

Getting to Banff   Calgary is the nearest international airport, located 145 km (1.5 hours west). There are several shuttle options that service the Bow Valley, including the Banff Airporter. Expect to pay roughly $70 for a one-way ticket.

Hostels   Hostelling International (HI) members save 10 percent. You *absolutely* want to book all stops in advance at hihostels.ca. Also, check availability before committing to any one location. Locations of indoor accommodation options en route follow.

0 km	Banff (hostel and $$$ lodges)
31 km	Castle Junction (hostel and $$$ lodge)
46 km	Baker Creek ($$$ lodge)
59 km	Lake Louise (hostel and $$$ lodges)
87 km	Mosquito Creek (hostel)
151 km	Rampart Creek (hostel)
206 km	Beauty Creek (rustic hostel)
259 km	Athabasca Falls (hostel)
292 km	Jasper (hostel and $$$ lodges)

Ideal Window   All restock points between Lake Louise and Jasper are closed between November and April. If you are starting in March, please note also that from March 1 to June 25, travel is not permitted between 8:00 p.m. and 8:00 a.m. on the 17-km stretch of the Bow Valley Parkway from the Fireside Picnic Area near Banff to the Johnston Canyon Campground (so as not to disrupt nocturnal animal traffic). To get the most from the adventure, try to time your ride with some of the exciting events happening in the area, such as the world-renowned Banff Mountain Film and Book Festival (banffcentre.ca/banff-mountain-film-book-festival) in early November.

North to south or south to north?   Tour companies often shuttle to Jasper to begin the ride (none operate in winter). For paying clients, it is nice to get the more than four-hour van ride out of the way first. If you look at the elevation gain/loss, however, it makes more sense to ride south to north. Having also completed a "yo-yo" of the route (down and back) in February

2017, I can attest to less hike-a-bike on my very snowy and icy ride when northbound. On the reverse, the climb up to Brewster's Skywalk (6 km before the Columbia Icefield, en route to Sunwapta Pass) is particularly challenging in icy conditions.

Pacing   When considering how many kilometres to aim for each day, keep in mind that your average speed could be in the 5–10 km/h range. My longest continuous stretch was 172 km, and it took 16 hours to complete, not including breakfast and getting packed at 4:00 a.m. Like all routes, if this itinerary seems too ambitious, plan your trip accordingly.

Phone coverage   Cell coverage is good in Banff, Castle Junction, Lake Louise, Athabasca Falls and Jasper. It is spotty to non-existent everywhere else. That said, almost all rest stops, which are more frequent in Jasper National Park, have pay phones that accept credit cards or can call collect.

Road closures   Periodically during winter, officials close the Icefields Parkway (for up to three days) to clear avalanches or take measures to prevent them. The problem area is between Rampart Creek and Beauty Creek Hostel. There are barriers at both ends of the Parkway, as well as at Saskatchewan Crossing. If those are closed, both motorized vehicles and cyclists are not permitted past them. A variety of winter travel resources can be found at pc.gc.ca/en/pn-np/ab/banff/visit/brochures#winter. You can also follow @511 on Twitter for real-time updates.

Shuttle back   Sundog Tours (sundogtours.com) is the primary bus company operating in the winter, running October to April, costing $79 from Jasper to Banff plus $30 for your bike (must be boxed). An additional $56 to go all the way to the Calgary International Airport. Be prepared for delays in inclement weather. Bus pilots are at the whim of road conditions, the same as everyone else.

Traffic   This is a very different highway than the one that can see thousands of vehicles per month through July and August. Expect to see only a handful of vehicles every hour, carrying a mixture of workers passing through, park wardens, ice climbers, skiers, Ski Doo enthusiasts and the occasional tourist. The road is closed year-round to commercial semi traffic. Please also note that the lanes of traffic (and shoulder) will often be difficult to distinguish. Keep your head on a swivel.

Warden stations   There is a warden station 2 km south of the highway junction at Saskatchewan Crossing. There's another at Sunwapta, at the trailhead for Poboktan Creek Trail (14 km north of Beauty Creek). Both may be in various states of decommission. In case of emergency, you are better off depending on passing vehicles.

Wild and traditional camping   There are only two winter campgrounds

directly on route. Wapiti, just south of Jasper, which is more established, and Wilcox, near the Columbia Icefield, possibly decommissioned and maybe buried under a metre of snow. Wild camping is not permitted anywhere in the national park corridor. Again, I strongly encourage you to choose the hostel approach. Camping is not a viable plan.

Day 1: Banff to Lake Louise (59 km)

Venture west along the Bow Valley Parkway for what is largely a front-country warm-up to the Icefields Parkway. This is your opportunity to take advantage of available restock points, hot hostel showers and good cell reception. No substantial challenges to concern yourself with today. Get a feel for your rig, your body and how both are adjusting to the elements.

BANFF RECOMMENDATIONS

Banff is a full-services mountain town – 4 million visitors (and growing) pass through the national park each year. Learn more at banff.ca.

Java fix The Wildflour Bakery (wildflourbakery.ca) is a tremendous stop for handcrafted espresso drinks, homemade breads, soups and tasty treats. There are two locations: 101-211 Bear Street is the flagship stop, open 8:00 a.m. to 4:00 p.m. daily.

Sleep on the cheap The Banff International Hostel (banffinternationalhostel.com) is within walking distance of all services. Approximately $36/night. Just be wary of European travellers who may invite you out on a pub crawl. Do not claim to be able to "drink them under the table" or you will spend the next two days in the fetal position. True story.

Stock up Head on over to the IGA at 318 Marten Street. Open 8:00 a.m. to 11:00 p.m. daily.

Transit between Canmore and Banff If your travels begin here, please note that Banff Legacy Trail (between Canmore and Banff) is *unsafe* to ride in the winter. It is also gated in a few locations. Check out Roam Regional Transit instead (roamtransit.com). They have carriers for your bike. A one-way fare to Banff is $6 cash. You could also take on the groomed Goat Creek back route. Check trail conditions first. It is a slog in fresh snow.

*Additional Banff recommendations can be found in the High Rockies route (chapter 2).

0 km	Begin at the Banff Visitor Centre on Banff Avenue. Open 9:00 a.m.–5:00 p.m. daily. Head north and take your first left on Wolf Street. In three blocks, turn right on Lynx Street and follow it out of town.
1.7 km	Turn left on the Trans-Canada Highway to head west. Follow signs for Lake Louise. You are on the busy road for 6 km. There is a good shoulder when plowed. Be especially careful in fresh snow conditions.
7.2 km	Turn right on Highway 1A. Keep right, heading under the log-beam entrance for the Bow Valley Parkway. Follow signs for Lake Louise.
24.9 km	Johnston Canyon Campground (closed for season). Johnston Canyon Resort (also closed) is just ahead on the right. Take on the 2.6-km hike to the upper falls for a great picture opportunity.
31.2 km	Castle Junction.

CASTLE JUNCTION RECOMMENDATIONS

Restock The general store at the junction corner, part of Castle Mountain Chalets (castlemountain.com) is open year-round. Make sure to grab an apple fritter at the front counter. They are fresh delivered from Fergie's Bakery in Canmore.

Sleep on the cheap Your stay at Castle Mountain Wilderness Hostel includes hot showers, cell coverage, a bike rack and linens. Approximately $30/night. Great little stop if you are running short on daylight. Book in advance at hihostels.ca.

45.6 km	Cross Baker Creek.

BAKER CREEK MOUNTAIN RESORT

Baker Creek Mountain Resort (bakercreek.com) is open year-round. $$$ chalets and licensed Cabin Cafe. Primarily a dinner stop. Formal dress not required.

52.8 km	"Morant's Curve." Tremendous view of the Bow River, CP railway and surrounding mountains.
56.9 km	Turn left at a junction to head down toward the hamlet of Lake Louise (right goes to ski resort). Cross back over the Trans-Canada Highway.
58 km	At a four-way stop for Village Road, turn right. Shopping plaza and multiple convenience stores on every corner. Continue across Pipestone River bridge.
58.5 km	Lake Louise Alpine Centre hostel. The largest and most modern of the hostels along the Icefields Parkway. Open 24 hours. Hot showers, WiFi, bike rack, linens, shared kitchen and the licensed Bill Peyto's Cafe on site. Approximately $40/night. Book online at hihostels.ca. Double-check Icefields Parkway road conditions this evening. This is your last opportunity to rebook hostels ahead.

LAKE LOUISE RECOMMENDATIONS (EVENING)

Most services are within a block of Samson Mall. Learn more at banfflakelouise.com.

Energy to burn?   The road up to Moraine Lake is closed to traffic in the winter but groomed and open to fat bikers. Your next-best tourist diversion is a 4-km climb to the Chateau Lake Louise, where the deli is open 24 hours a day. They have coffee, picnic lunches, all that good stuff. Option three: take a jaunt along the original 1A highway. The 20-km out-and-back track begins on your right, en route to the Chateau. There's a "Great Divide" sign at the turnoff. A full listing of local winter trails can be found at pc.gc.ca/en/pn-np/ab/banff/visit/brochures#winter.

Restock   The Village Market is the only dedicated grocery store in the area. Buy enough to get you to Jasper, and perhaps a bit more. Be prepared for those "what if?" scenarios.

Tune up   Wilson's Mountain Sports (wmsll.com) can provide basic bike service (they focus on rentals). Open 9:00 a.m. to 7:00 p.m. daily. The shop has been around for over 20 years.

Day 2: Lake Louise to Rampart Creek (91 km)

Your day begins with a gradual 44-km ascent of Bow Pass. Behold the grand glacier valley.

LAKE LOUISE RECOMMENDATIONS (MORNING)

Java fix   Laggan's Mountain Bakery (laggans.com) is a quick-service favourite in Samson Mall. Open 7:00 a.m. to 6:00 p.m. daily. Enjoy a morning trifecta of baked goods, breakfast and hot coffee.

0 km	Backtrack to the Trans-Canada Highway. The pedestrian path that cyclists can use to bypass the highway (the opposite direction on Village Road) is not plowed in the winter.
0.9 km	Turn left on the Trans-Canada to head west toward Jasper. Carefully navigate the highway shoulder for the next 2.6 km.
3.5 km	Turn right on Highway 93 (the Icefields Parkway). The Banff National Park pass booth is in 500 m, a good opportunity to ask about travel conditions. Begin climbing to Bow Pass.
22.4 km	Hector Lake viewpoint.

PHOTO: JEFF BARTLETT

27.4 km	Mosquito Creek Hostel on your left. Approximately $27/night. Book in advance at hihostels.ca. Linens, shared kitchen and wood sauna on site.
37.7 km	Bow Lake viewpoint. Here are the headwaters of the Bow River, flowing down through Canmore and on to Calgary and beyond.
39.1 km	Turn off for Num-Ti-Jah Lodge (closed for the season).
43.8 km	Top out at Bow Pass, elevation 2070 m. Coming in behind Highwood Pass, it is the second-highest paved climb in all of Canada. Begin the net downhill to Saskatchewan Crossing.
77.6 km	Warden station is on your right. Continue over the North Saskatchewan River.
79.5 km	Continue straight at Highway 11 junction. Saskatchewan Crossing Resort is just ahead (closed for season). Gradual climb from here to Rampart Creek.
91.6 km	Rampart Creek Hostel on your right. Approximately $27/night. Book in advance at hihostels.ca. Linens provided. Wood sauna also on site.

Day 3: Rampart Creek to Athabasca Falls (108 km)

Much like yesterday's start, the route climbs for the first 33 km to Sunwapta Pass. Notice the first substantial kick at 18 km, then again after Big Bend (self explanatory once you are in it). The view back down the Icefields Parkway is one of the most photographed.

Up top, the Columbia Icefield is devoid of the normal high-season tourism bustle. Enjoy an uninterrupted view of Athabasca Glacier before beginning the lengthy net downhill to Athabasca Falls.

0 km	Continue north along Highway 93.
15.7 km	Look for water trickling down the vertical limestone on your right, a unique face called the Weeping Wall.
18.2 km	The first kick up, toward the bridge over Nigel Falls.
21.7 km	Circle around Big Bend and begin second kick up the Sunwapta. Good views back down the valley within the next kilometre.
29.5 km	Hilda Creek Hostel (closed for season) is up the hill to your left.
32.2 km	Top out at an elevation of 2062 m. Sunwapta is the fourth-highest paved climb in Canada. You'll see a sign for Jasper National Park ahead on the left as you start down. There is a high likelihood of blowing snow over the next 10 km.
34.8 km	Wilcox Creek Campground. Open but likely buried under snow. Make sure to pack out all your garbage.

37.7 km	The Columbia Icefield Discovery Centre is on your right (closed for season). This high mountain region is a hydrogeological apex. Water from the melting Columbia Icefield flows to the Pacific, the Arctic and the Atlantic oceans.
42.5 km	Short climb up to Brewster Skywalk (closed for season). There's a lengthier 4-km descent on the other side. Keep an eye out for Triangle Falls within the first kilometre, a popular spot for ice climbers.
48.1 km	Bottom out. The Sunwapta River runs through this valley. It was one of the more accessible water sources on my first winter scout.
54.8 km	Beauty Creek Hostel on your left. Approximately $27/night. Rustic location that *must* be booked in advance at hihostels.ca. After booking, you receive a code for the locked door, plus instruction on how to ignite the propane appliances. This hostel does not have a manager on site.
69 km	Pass over Poboktan Creek. On your right is the Sunwapta warden station.
86 km	Sunwapta Falls Resort (closed for season) is on your left. The Sunwapta Falls overlook is 1 km west from this junction.
108.6 km	Athabasca Hostel is on your right. Approximately $27/night. Linens and a shared kitchen. Bonus (depending on who you ask): a pocket of cell service. Book in advance at hihostels.ca.

Day 4: Athabasca Falls to Jasper (33 km)

Enjoy a relaxed rolling finish through the Marmot Basin to Jasper.

0 km	Continue north along Highway 93.
0.7 km	Highway 93A junction (closed in winter). The Athabasca Falls overlook is 500 m off route. Be careful of your footing along the icy walkways.
6.6 km	Athabasca Pass overlook. This is the high point of today's route.
23.3 km	Bridge over the Athabasca River.
27.5 km	Wapiti Campground is on your right. This is the one other tent site that is open in winter. Book in advance at reservation.pc.gc.ca.

30.1 km	Cross the Miette River and continue straight through the ensuing stoplight. Highway 93 turns into Connaught Avenue as it curves east through Jasper.
32.7 km	Turn left on Miette Avenue. Finish at the Jasper Information Centre, a National Historic Site (in the park on your right), open 9:00 a.m. to 5:00 p.m. daily.

JASPER RECOMMENDATIONS

Jasper is the tourism hub for the surrounding national park. Learn more at jasper.travel.

Got an extra day? Jasper is starting to actively promote itself as a fat biking destination. Connect with a local bike shop or trailforks.com for current trail conditions.

Java fix The Bear's Paw Bakery (bearspawbakery.com) is a fixture of my rides along the Icefields Parkway. Open 6:00 a.m. to 6:00 p.m. daily. Grab a homemade cinnamon bun! Coffee roasted at Bean Around the World in North Vancouver. SnowDome Coffee Bar (snowdome.coffee) is another go-to for locals and also houses a laundromat. Open Sunday through Tuesday, 7:00 a.m. to 5:00 p.m.; Wednesday through Saturday, 7:00 a.m. to 8:00 p.m.

Need to box your bike? Vicious Cycle (viciouscanada.com) and The Bench Bike Shop (thebenchbikeshop.com) can help get you sorted for the return trip.

Sleep on the cheap The new HI Jasper hostel on Sleepy Hollow Road is a modern and comfortable option just a short walk from downtown. Hot showers, linens, shared kitchen, and café. Book in advance at hihostels.ca. If you're travelling in a group, it might also be nice to split a hotel room. Treat yourself!

APPENDICES

A. Ultralight Packing List

The gear list below is an ideal starting point for longer-mileage days in the mountains. Remember, bikepacking strives for a lightweight approach.

WEARING

- Base layer
- Bib shorts
- Breathable long-finger gloves
- Cheapo watch
- Cycling cap
- Flexible, clipless shoes or hiking boots
- Helmet with headlight
- Jersey with food in pockets
- Polarized sunglasses
- Higher-cut socks
- Whistle around neck

MOUNTAIN BIKE MODIFICATIONS

The gold standard is a 29er hardtail for most any ride listed in this guidebook. Consider using the following:

- Aero bars
- Ergonomic grips with extra cork grip tape
- Friction tape for bag rub points
- Platform (flat) pedals
- Rigid carbon front fork (more so for racing on non-technical terrain)
- Tubeless wheelset with sealant

TECHNOLOGY

- Dynamo hub on front wheel
- Dynamo-powered front light
- GPS device

- Satellite tracker
- Smartphone
- usb power bank(s)
- usb power switch

SADDLE BAG

You may want to further organize with sublists for Layers and Peripheral items. Waterproof material is ideal for all bags.

- Buff
- Second pair of bib shorts
- Second pair of warmer, long-finger gloves
- Second, warmer base layer
- Skull cap
- Warm middle layer
- Waterproof shell jacket
- Wool socks

HANDLEBAR PACK

I generally reserve the space in the handlebar pack for camp-setup gear. Pack the following items assuming you can find relatively comfortable ground, sheltered from the elements. Nixing a Thermarest yields a considerable space saving. Use pine needles and long grass instead.

- Bivouac sack
- Sleeping bag

ACCESSORIES POCKET

- Batteries and chargers for gadgets
- Guidebook and/or paper maps
- List of emergency numbers
- Passport
- Small food items
- Small toothbrush and toothpaste
- Wallet
- Wet wipes
- Ziploc bags for organizing

FRONT TOP TUBE PACK

- Electrolyte capsules
- Small food items
- Smartphone

REAR TOP TUBE PACK

- Acid reflux tabs
- Anti-inflammatory drugs
- Chamois cream
- Lighter
- Lip balm
- Small knife
- Sunscreen
- Water purification tablets

HANDLEBAR FOOD POUCHES

- Small food items
- Water bottles

FRAME PACK

Due to frame triangle space varying between bikes, this is the one bag that bikepackers often get custom built. Ziploc bags are, again, going to come in handy here for organizing smaller items.

- A few zip ties
- Chain breaker
- Duct tape (wrapped around seat post)
- First-aid items
- High-volume pump
- Larger food items
- Multitool
- Needle and thread for tire
- Patch kit
- Quick links
- Sidewall boot
- Ski strap(s)
- Small rag
- Spare brake pads
- Spare cleat bolts
- Spare spoke
- Spare water bladder
- Spare-tire sealant
- Tire lever
- Two tubes
- Wet or dry lube

B. Creature Comforts

Planning to stop more often and enjoy the view? Including the following gear will make for more of a comfortable touring experience.

Backpack Good for carrying extra food, water and quickly accessible items like a nice camera and spare layer. Just be conscious that the extra weight will transfer to your shoulders and saddle. You want to train with this load in advance.

Bear spray What animal deterrents you should have on hand is a highly debated topic. Some may consider bear spray a mandatory item, and in the book I note some places where I believe it is mandatory.

Extra layers Including regular clothes for walking around town, rain pants and more variations on the standard kit.

Inflatable pillow Another option would be to stuff clothing in your backpack.

Reading material There is nothing like catching up on a good book after a long day of riding.

Sandals Allow your feet to breathe as you walk around camp (for quicker recovery of blisters) or to dangle in a cool creek. Sandals are also handy in grimy campsite showers.

Stove, pot and fuel The ability to cook freeze-dried and whole-food meals = fuelling variety that often yields longer-lasting satiation. Simple carbohydrates often associated with convenience-store bikepacker diets are a quick-burn calorie source.

Thermarest Saves you the hassle of trying to find a comfortable space to set up camp. Also reduces heat lost through conduction with the ground and gives you a better-quality sleep.

Ultralight tent The ability to sit up and change in comfort, store items out of the elements and not have moisture collect in your sleeping bag (as it often does in a bivouac) are all good things. You can strap the tent poles to your downtube if need be.

C. Winter Gear Considerations

Bottle insulation Start by pouring warm water into a standard bottle or bladder. You then want to shelter it from the wind by either placing it in one of your bags and/or using a specially designed bottle cover. Neoprene material works well. You also want to shake your bottles every hour to break up any frozen chunks. Use bottles with larger lids. Small spray spouts usually freeze.

PHOTO: MATTHEW CLARK

Fat bike with studded tires   Don't chance a winter tour with a traditional mountain bike. Even the friendliest of conditions can yield snow and ice at a moment's notice. You want to be prepared for the storm, not the relatively clear asphalt, ahead.

Hand and toe warmers   Always a good idea in temperatures under –10°C and for people with circulation issues, like Raynaud's.

Plastic pedals   Unlike metal pedals, plastic ones do not pull heat away from the bottom of your shoes. Of course, this may negate the use of clipless boots.

Pogies   Large overmitts that insulate your hands from the wind. You still want to carry warm gloves, though they might not be necessary while riding.

Riding boots   Special clipless boots are a must for racing types. Traditional winter boots work fine for the average touring cyclist.

Ski helmet and goggles   For the most extreme temperatures, this combo is sure to keep your head warm and eyes free from wind and glare.

Winter riding pants   Tapered pants that keep your legs warm and maintain a normal range of motion. A bib short underneath is still a good idea to minimize chafing.

D. Regional Events

I have only listed local Canadian Rocky Mountain events that, in true bikepacking spirit, carry no entry fee, award no prizes and are totally self-supported.

ALBERTA ROCKIES 700

A 700-km loop beginning and ending in Canmore, Alberta. The grand depart is in August. albertarockies700.com.

BC EPIC

The original epic is 1000 km across southern British Columbia. You can also test your mettle at the shorter Buckshot event. Grand depart is from Merritt, British Columbia, in June. bcepic1000.com.

THE LOST ELEPHANT (FORMERLY KOOTENAY GRAVEL GRINDER)

The 500-km "Jumbo" circumnavigates the East Kootenays. The shorter "Dumbo" route is approximately 320 km. Grand depart is from Cranbrook, British Columbia, in July. lostelephant.ca.

TOUR DIVIDE

4418 km from Banff, Alberta, to Antelope Wells, New Mexico. Grand depart is the second Friday of June. tourdivide.org.

*In the east, Ontario now has some exciting bikepacking events to check out, including the popular 700 km BT700 and the 350 km GNR. Information about both is available at bt700.ca.

E. Helpful Links

Delve deeper into the world of bikepacking, both in the Rocky Mountains and abroad. More-specific links are included within each route.

COMMUNITY

Bikepack Canada   Hub for Canadian bikepackers, including a podcast, monthly newsletter, overnighter rides and an annual summit in Canmore. bikepack.ca.

Bikepacking.com   Inspired routes and reviews. bikepacking.com.

Bikepacking.net   The original forum for all things bikepacking. bikepacking.net.

Adventure Cycling Association A tremendous resource for route maps. They also produce an engaging magazine that covers touring stories (road and off-road) from around the world. adventurecycling.org.

EVENT COVERAGE

Track Leaders Satellite-tracking site for events using SPOT and DeLorme devices. trackleaders.com.

MTB Cast Rider call-ins are posted to the web for followers back home. An engaging way to hear our stories in real-time. mtbcast.com.

ROCKY MOUNTAIN PUBLIC LANDS

Alberta Provincial Parks Reserve campsites, review trail reports and animal advisories and more. albertaparks.ca.

Alberta Environment and Parks Gain an understanding of Public Land Use Zones (PLUZ) and snow/rainfall levels in the river basins. alberta.ca/public-land-use-zones.aspx.

British Columbia Provincial Parks Reserve campsites, review trail reports and animal advisories and more. bcparks.ca.

National Parks of Canada Reserve campsites, purchase backcountry permits and explore a full listing of legal cycling routes. pc.gc.ca.

NAVIGATION

The Great Trail Also known as the Trans Canada Trail, the Great Trail is the longest recreational path in the world. Download the app for extra navigation on the sections we utilize. thegreattrail.ca.

Trailforks Community-driven database of mountain bike routes. Along with Google Maps, this can be a good resource for linking your own overnighter routes. trailforks.com.

TRAVEL SERVICES

HI Hostels Before booking any hostel, make sure to sign up for an annual membership to receive a discounted rate on each stay. With the membership, you also save on car rentals and other travel discounts. hihostels.ca.

ACKNOWLEDGEMENTS

The wheels for this project were set in motion by pioneers who came long before me. First, thank you to Michael "Mac" McCoy and the Adventure Cycling Association for plotting the Great Divide Route in the early 1990s.

To the race pioneers, a special thank you to Mountain Bike Hall of Fame rider John Stamstad for being the first to ITT (individual time trial) from border to border in 1999. To Mike Curriak for instigating the first grand depart along that same route in 2014. And then to Matthew Lee for rebranding the experience with the Tour Divide in 2008. It is important to remember that there was a time when only a handful of bikepackers showed up to a start line, and none yet referred to it as bikepacking.

Speaking of which, thank you to Jill Homer for opening my eyes to the scene in 2009.

Not long after that, Mike Dion's documentary *Ride the Divide* caught fire, inspiring the next generation of riders to send in their letters of intent, buy those novel canvas bags and venture forth to Banff. Thanks, dude!

To my wife, Sarah, thank you for being my support on all the scouts. Too often I left you waiting, waiting and waiting some more (and guessing my state of distress) for my tracking dot to come down off the mountain. Thank you also for your patience during the writing phase. It has been a selfish process with the most unselfish of intentions. I love you.

Mom and Dad, raising a headstrong teenager is perhaps the greatest adventure of all. Thank you for knowing when to push, pull or just let go.

And finally, I would like to say a very special thank you to the following individuals for coming on board as guidebook sponsors: Greg Van Tighem, Guy Stuart, Joanne Maurice, Jacqueline Campbell, Penny Lawless, Sam Campbell, Michael Hill, Tracy Watkin, Ben Ritman and Terry Stone. Your support allowed me the extra time to write and explore (and replace that lost SPOT tracker).

On to the next extraordinary adventure.

— **RYAN CORREY**

Ryan Correy was one of Canada's most accomplished adventure cyclists. In addition to writing about these adventures in two books, *A Purpose Ridden* and *Bikepacking in the Canadian Rockies*, Ryan regularly spoke to professional groups about turning passion into purpose and was actively involved in various forms of charity work. He was also the founder of Bikepack Canada (bikepack.ca) and was a tireless promoter of cycling and outdoor adventure. Ryan died in April 2018 after a courageous battle with cancer.